D1446549

Diary of a Rich Man's Kid

Diary of a
Rich Man's Kid

Charles Pettijohn Jr.

BEAUFORT
BOOKS

BEAUFORT BOOKS
NEW YORK

Copyright © 2014 by Charles C. Pettijohn

FIRST EDITION

All rights reserved. No part of this book may be reproduced
in any form or by any electronic or mechanical means, including information storage and retrieval systems, without permission in writing from the publisher, except by a
reviewer who may quote brief passages in a review.

All photos are Pettijohn Family photos unless otherwise noted.
Photo credits: p.88 Corbis

Library of Congress Cataloging-in-Publication Data
Pettijohn, Charles C., Jr.
Diary of a rich man's kid : old Hollywood, world leaders, movers &
shakers, and one boy at the center of it all! / Charles C. Pettijohn, Jr.
pages cm
ISBN 978-0-8253-0731-7 (pbk. : alk. paper)
1. Pettijohn, Charles C., Jr. 2. Hollywood (Los Angeles,
Calif.)--History--Anecdotes. 3. Hollywood (Los
Angeles, Calif.)--History--Biography. 4. Motion pic-
ture industry--California--Los Angeles. I. Title.
F869.H74P48 2014   384'.80979494--dc23.................2013048135

For inquiries about volume orders, please contact:
Beaufort Books
27 West 20th Street, Suite 1102
New York, NY 10011
sales@beaufortbooks.com

Published in the United States by Beaufort Books
www.beaufortbooks.com

Distributed by Midpoint Trade Books
www.midpointtrade.com

Printed in the United States of America

Book design by Jamie Kerry of Belle Étoile Studios
Cover design by Michael Short

Contents

INTRODUCTION   9

Part 1: Family And Early Life

1	Family	17
2	Adventures in Youth	27
3	Trip to Europe	37
4	Politics	53
5	Sports	67

Part 2: Adventures in California

| 6 | Toluca Lake | 79 |
| 7 | Lakeside Stories | 83 |

Part 3: Career

8	Film and Early Career	105
9	The Navy	111
10	Television	120

11 Drinking Stories   138
12 Red Skelton   146
13 Carol Burnett   150

    A FINAL NOTE FROM ADRIENNE   156

    ABOUT THE AUTHORS   160

Diary of a Rich Man's Kid

Introduction

THE MARCH 25, 2011 edition of the entertainment publication, *The Hollywood Reporter*, featured an article entitled, "80 Years of *The Hollywood Reporter*." The article was about Hal Roach, producer of the *Laurel & Hardy* and *Our Gang* film series in the 1930s, creating a film studio partnership with Italian dictator Benito Mussolini in 1937. The story's photo featured Hal Roach and Vittorio Mussolini, Benito's son, aboard a ship traveling from Italy to New York. There was a third person in the photo — my grandfather, Charles Pettijohn. The photo looked awfully familiar because I'd seen it many times in my father's family photo album. But unlike the photo in *The Hollywood Reporter*, the one I'd seen in my father's album was autographed ... by Vittorio Mussolini.

This prompted me to resurrect the book manuscript my father had started after he retired from CBS Television Network in the mid-1970s. Titled, *Diary of a Rich Man's Kid*, Dad described his upbringing by parents who were involved in politics, sports, and the film industry.

My grandfather, part Cherokee Indian, was born in Indianapolis on May 5, 1881. A one-time baseball player, he worked his way through Indiana University Law School, graduating in 1903. In 1913, he became Deputy Prosecutor and City Attorney of Indianapolis, then head of the Democratic Party for the State of Indiana. Among his political associates was Joseph Kennedy, and their families were very close. Other close friends included the Roosevelt family, J. Edgar Hoover, President Herbert Hoover (no relation to J. Edgar), and some international government leaders who you'll read about later. An article in New Rochelle, NY's the *Standard-Star* newspaper described him as:

> A man to whom a collar means nothing; a man who has no extravagances, is temperate but not a teetotaler, likes to travel, welcomes foreign assignments (has about one a year) and above all, loves children. Every Saturday and Sunday you can find him surrounded by 300 to 500 children at Pettijohn Park which he built. Children flock around him because he talks to them, plays with them, and brings others to see them. When Vittorio Mussolini was here (in Westchester N.Y.) he and Mr. Pettijohn visited the park. How the youngsters of Italian parentage thrilled to that. On Decoration Day, Mr. Pettijohn pitched, and Jimmy Cagney, film star, caught in the softball game. It was a great day for the youngsters. Following the World War, he and ex-president Herbert Hoover raised more than 21 million dollars for the starving children of Europe.

My grandfather's involvement in the motion picture industry began in 1914 when he defended a group of motion picture exhibitors. Ultimately, he became General Counsel for the Motion Picture Association of America. Among his motion picture associates were Lewis J. Selznick, Louis B. Mayer, and Cecil B. DeMille. He married Helen Lynch. They had two children: my father, Charles, and his younger brother, Bruce. Bruce Pettijohn became the youngest law student to receive a PhD in that discipline. He grew up to become the Attorney General for the State of New York.

My father, Charles C. Pettijohn II, was born in New York in 1918. His mom taught him to play golf, and he hit his first hole-in-one by age ten. His golf talent was exhibited in competitions throughout his years at Rye Country Day School, Portsmouth Priory, and Georgetown University. The July 15, 1935 issue of the *New York Sun* featured an article about my father as a golf prodigy.

"Charlie grew up here on the Westchester grounds … David Selznick, the movie mogul, gave Charles a toy set of golf sticks on Christmas when he was just 4 years old … Charlie was just born to be a golfer … because he picked up the game instinctively and developed rapidly without ever taking a real lesson … Charlie broke 100 when only 8 years old. At eleven he cracked 90 and at 14 he broke 80 … "

Dad's stories describe his experiences with political legends such as President Roosevelt and Joe Kennedy, foreign leaders such as Benito Mussolini and King

Edward VIII of England, sports legends such as Babe Ruth and Joe DiMaggio, historical legends such as J. Edgar Hoover and John Dillinger, and entertainment celebrities such as Clark Gable, Bob Hope, and Cher, just to name a few. My father became a bit of a celebrity himself. But I'll leave that for you to discover as you read his "diary." If some of the stories seem rather unbelievable, I hope the photographs dispel any doubts.

Enjoy,
Adrienne Pettijohn

*Charles Pettijohn Sr, Vittorio Mussolini and
Hal Roach aboard the S.S. Rex*

PART 1

Family And Early Life

CHAPTER 1

Family

Me and Dad

WITH VERY FEW exceptions, kids are dumb. I was not an exception. I was also a rich man's kid, and rich men's kids are dumber than poor men's kids. Don't believe me? Look around you. Now by "rich" I don't mean like the Rockefellers or the Vanderbilts. But Dad had a very good position, a large salary, a home beside a golf course in Westchester County, New York, and a summer cottage on a lake in

Connecticut, with a speed boat and a tennis court. But we never quite got into polo. I sometimes worried about what I wanted to eat, but never about from where the next meal was coming.

Dad also knew every important person in the world, or at least everyone I thought was important. And I got to meet them all, but was too dumb to know it at the time. I'll tell you about them in a while, but first I have to tell you about Dad because he was the most important. And, of course, being dumb, I didn't know that at the time either.

Dad worked his way through the University of Indiana, then law school. He got involved in politics, and quickly became the District Attorney of Indianapolis. He left Indiana and went to New York City, where he somehow became the attorney for L. J. Selznick, the movie producer. Selznick was making lots of money, but spending it even faster.

He wanted to own the whole movie business himself. Dad told him movies were going to be a big business, and that there was room for everybody. He told Selznick to just concentrate on making his own films. Selznick refused to do so. Dad resigned. No use paying a lawyer for advice if the client won't take it. Dad left. But before he left, he went into Selznick's safe and stole a quarter of a million dollars in cash. He then walked down the street to the Corn Exchange Bank, rented a safety deposit box, and put the money in it. Selznick never missed it.

Dad then went around to all the other producers. They all hated the distributors and exhibitors. And they hated each other, too. Dad insisted that films were going to become a big industry and would have industrial problems like any other big industry. They should form an association of their own to deal with their common problems. They should all put a buck in the hat and start this association. It would be a lot cheaper than paying lawyers to fight their common problems and themselves, too. They said, "NO!"

Then came the Black Sox scandal in the World Series. The baseball club owners liked each other about as much as the producers liked each other, but they saw the light. They all put a buck in the hat, and hired a commissioner to tell them what to do. He was Supreme Court Justice Kenesaw Mountain Landis. He soon became known as the Czar of Baseball. The producers were impressed. They liked the word *czar*, and wanted one of their own. They held a meeting, and gave Dad two weeks to find them a czar. Dad came back with two names: Herbert Hoover, Secretary of Commerce, and Will Hays, the Chairman of the Republican Party and Postmaster General in President Harding's cabinet. The producers picked Hays. Hoover disappeared into obscurity and later reappeared as President of the United States.

The organization was called The Motion Picture Producers and Distributors of America, Inc. Dad became the General Council. He handled any legislation that might affect the motion picture industry unfavorably.

About two years went by, and Dad went to see L. J. Selznick. He was living in a walk-up apartment on

Amsterdam Avenue. He had gone bankrupt and was flat broke. They got on a street car and went downtown to the Corn Exchange Bank. Dad opened the lock box and gave Selznick back his quarter of a million dollars. Selznick thanked Dad and paid him three dollars for the rent on the lock box. He then went back into business and soon made another fortune. His two sons were not dumb. First they had been a rich man's kids, then a poor man's kids, and then rich again. They learned from both sides. And they did well. Myron became the top talent agent in Hollywood. David became a producer. You may remember *Gone with the Wind*. It was pretty damn good.

* * *

I've told you a lot about Dad, so now I want to tell you about Mom. She was born in Boston, and her name was Helen Irene Lynch. At sixteen she left home to go on the stage. Her Dad had died when she was twelve, and her mother had gone back to teaching in an elementary school. She had a younger brother, Jimmy, and a younger sister, Blanche, who became one of the original Gibson Girls on the New York stage. Mom always sent some money home whenever she got paid for acting. Her stage name was Belle Bruce. She got into silent pictures and became a movie star before she was twenty years old. Her best picture was *The Battle Cry of Peace*. Then she met Dad and married him. When I was born she quit making movies. I guess she had her hands full with me.

Mom

*Frank E. Merriman (Governor of California),
Cecil B. DeMille (standing), Gary Cooper, and Mom*

Me and Uncle Jimmy

Mom's little brother, my Uncle Jimmy, decided to become a baseball player. He made it to the major leagues, where he pitched for both the Chicago Cubs and the Boston Red Sox. He took time out when he enlisted in the Army for World War I and became an ambulance driver in France.

During the off-season, Uncle Jimmy used to keep in shape by pitching to Mom. She was the only woman I ever knew who owned her own catcher's mitt. I was very, very proud of her. She also taught me how to pitch. When I was in the eighth grade, we had a father and son game at Rye Country Day School. None of the fathers would catch behind the bat. So Mom had to catch for them. Uncle Jimmy taught me how to throw a change-up, and I saved it for the father and son game. I wanted to use it on Dad. I did. He hit it over the fence for a home run. It went all the way across the Boston Post Road. Obviously, I should have worked on the pitch some more before throwing it in a game.

Mom and me

Mom was really good at sports. She taught me how to play golf when I was five years old. By the time I was nine, I could break a hundred, and I'd made my first hole-in-one. Sometimes Mom and I played golf with George Ruppert. He was the brother of Colonel Jacob Ruppert who owned the New York Yankees. He arranged for me to meet Babe Ruth. Mom and Uncle Jimmy took me to Yankee Stadium. We sat in the owner's box, right next to the Yankee dugout. Before the game, Babe came over and I had my picture taken with him. He told me he would hit a home run for me, and he did. I was the happiest eight-year-old kid on the face of the earth. Or maybe I had just died and gone to heaven.

Babe Ruth and me

Winsted And Uncle Jimmy

Uncle Jimmy liked to drink. So did his father-in-law, Mr. Clancy. Mom didn't like Uncle Jimmy drinking, and was quite adamant about it. One night at Winsted, Uncle Jimmy and Mr. Clancy told Mom they would take me for a ride in our motor boat. There was an amusement park at the other end of the lake and I thought they were going to let me ride on the roller coaster. But they didn't. They had another idea. A man named Flip managed the amusement park. He also had a still and made bootleg gin. Jimmy and Tom bought a bottle from Flip and stood on the dock drinking it. Suddenly Mr. Clancy coughed, said a word that sounded like "rotgut" and spit up into the lake. His false teeth came out and fell in the water.

We could see them lying on the bottom. The water was very cold, but Uncle Jimmy made me dive into the water anyway and recapture Mr. Clancy's teeth. I was soaking wet, and I was very cold going back to shore in the boat. Mother saw me. I looked like a drowned rat. She asked what happened and Uncle Jimmy told her I fell out of the boat. Mom bawled me out. She said if I wouldn't sit still in the boat she wouldn't let me ride in it anymore.

A year later I got even. It was November and very cold. One night Mom and Uncle Jimmy and I went for a ride in the boat. We were all bundled up in heavy clothes. In the middle of the lake the outboard motor stopped and I couldn't get it started. Uncle Jimmy told me to get out of the way and that he would start the motor. He wrapped the cord around the fly wheel, grabbed the handle, and gave it a gigantic tug. The handle came off and Jimmy fell out of the boat into the water. He sank. Suddenly his hat floated up. Then we heard Uncle Jimmy. His head was hitting the bottom of the boat. We pulled him up, and he held onto the side of the boat. He couldn't get into the boat without tipping it over. Mom told him to hold on to the back of the boat while I rowed it back to shore, towing him. The water was *very* cold but I rowed very slowly. I remembered Mr. Clancy's teeth falling into the water. When we finally got to shore, Uncle Jimmy looked like a drowned rat. I was glad, but I didn't say anything. Mom had seen it all in person ... it wasn't my fault.

Uncle Jimmy and his mom, my grandmother

CHAPTER 2

Adventures in Youth

Portsmouth Priory School

IN 1932, I finished the eighth grade at Rye Country Day School, thus completing my elementary education ... or so I thought. The Headmaster had a different thought. He told Mom and Dad that I would have to repeat the eighth grade. One of my classmates was Barnett Phillips III. He was the smartest boy in the class, and was a Catholic like me. His parents had enrolled him at Portsmouth Priory School in Newport, Rhode Island. He took the entrance exam, and he was so smart that they put him in the tenth grade instead of the ninth. Dad found out and somehow got me enrolled at Portsmouth Priory at the last minute. They put me in the tenth grade, too, because my education was the same as Barney's. This was a temporary measure until they could get my scholastic record from Rye Country Day School. Somehow they never got it. I suspect Dad's finger was somewhere in the pie.

Mom drove me up to Portsmouth as Dad was away on a campaign trip with FDR. September 17th was my birthday, and I received the following telegram which was sent care of Father Hugh Diman, the Prior. He called me to his office and handed me the telegram which he had already read. It went as follows: "Your Dad tells me this is your birthday and I want to wish a fine boy many happy returns." Signed, Franklin D. Roosevelt. The telegram sure helped, and I studied very hard. I got satisfactory marks in the first monthly examinations. My Rye Country Day School scholastic records were never mentioned again. I'm also forever grateful to Barney Phillips ... he was instrumental in my skipping a grade instead of repeating a grade. Come to think of it, I guess I skipped two grades. Thanks, Barney!

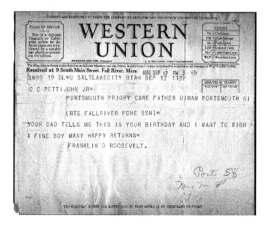

Telegram from FDR

Me golfing

Dr. Lally, a great horse lover, was my history teacher at Portsmouth. I was having trouble passing my history courses. Somehow, Dad had Kentucky Governor, Ruby Laffoon, make me a Kentucky Colonel. I had my commission framed and hung it on the wall in my room. Dr. Lally was impressed with it, and I told Dad. A week or so later, another Kentucky Colonel commission arrived at Portsmouth. Governor Laffoon had appointed another Colonel. The colonel was Dr. Lally. I passed history.

A few miles down the road from Portsmouth was the Wanumetonomy Golf Club. We would hitchhike back and forth when we wanted to play golf. Edmund Burke was the club pro, and he introduced me to his younger brother, Johnny, who went to Rogers High in Newport. We played golf together a lot, and he became my closest friend. Charlie Johnson was a plumber in Newport. He played golf at the club, and many times he gave us a ride back and forth to school. His son went to Rogers High with Johnny, but I never met him while I was at Portsmouth. Many years later, when I was working at CBS, he walked into the restaurant across the street from the studio. I introduced myself to him and told him about the rides his father had given me. Charlie had died. Soon after that his son had come to Hollywood, looking for work as an actor. I think he did very well. His name is Van Johnson. [1]

Mom, Dad, the Cars and the Price of Gas

Dad loved to buy cars. He had a Cadillac for himself and a Packard Roadster for Mom. When my brother Bruce and I turned sixteen, he bought us each a car. He also liked to trade in cars. Mom fell in love with her Packard and never wanted to trade it in. She would only accept a new car every three or four years. One year he bought a fifth car, claiming that George, our gardener, needed a car to pick up things for the garden.

---

[1] Van Johnson was a film and television actor best-known for his roles in *Thirty Seconds in Tokyo* and *Brigadoon*.

Me and Mom

My job was to keep the cars filled with gas. I always filled them up at a service station where Dad had a charge account. Once I forgot to fill Dad's Cadillac and he drove down to the station to fill it himself. This was the day that Dad learned that gas had gone from twelve cents a gallon to fourteen cents a gallon. He was furious, and said that inflation would destroy the country. He was so mad he sold George's Chevy. George didn't mind. When he needed things for the garden, he used Dad's Cadillac.

Mom loved her Packard because it was big. She always wanted to drive big things. One day Dad was able to arrange for Mom to drive a fire engine. She was really thrilled. Another time she was at the gas station when the tanker truck drove up. The truck driver got out and admired Mom's Packard. He said he had always wanted to drive a car like hers. Mom admired his tanker and said that she had always wanted to drive a truck like his. They made a deal. The truck driver drove Mom's Packard to the next gas station. She followed him in his tanker. It made them both very happy.

I should mention my first car. It was a Ford. Dad gave it to me on my sixteenth birthday. I had a date with a girl named Nancy Henefield, and couldn't wait to take her for a drive. I was driving up Purchase Street with my arm around Nancy. I forgot I had my arm around Nancy, so I put my other arm around her. The car steered itself across Purchase Street into a tree. Nancy and I cut our heads on the windshield. My door was jammed shut, so we had to get out Nancy's side. Somebody gave us a ride back to the house. Dad looked at our cut foreheads and asked if we were all right. We were. Dad was very happy. He told me that nobody ever learned how to drive a car until they had an accident. He was very pleased that I didn't kill myself having mine. He bought me a new Ford. I have never had another accident.

Dillinger

And now some things that happened to me. I caught John Dillinger. At least I think I did. Here's the story. See what *you* think.

Dad had taken me on a trip to Chicago. We went to the races at Arlington Park with J. Edgar Hoover, the head of the FBI. It was Thursday. Hoover could only stay for three races. He had to get back to Washington. Dad and I walked out to the gate with him, and on the way back we stopped at the paddock circle where they were walking the horses for the next race. An old handler was leading one of the horses around the circle. He looked at Dad, turned the horse over to a helper, and came over and asked Dad, "Ain't youse Charlie Pettijohn?" Dad said yes, and they started to talk. It seems that they had both been born in Noblesville, Indiana, and their families knew each other. They talked about mutual friends, but I didn't pay much attention until the handler mentioned John Dillinger, who had grown up in a town a couple of miles from Noblesville. I really paid attention when he started talking about Public Enemy Number One. He said he had seen Dillinger several times at the track. I asked why the cops didn't pick him up, and he said, "Dillinger is too hot. They're afraid of him." He went on to say that Dillinger could be picked up any Sunday at a movie theater on the south side. He always went to the double feature every Sunday. Dad and I went back to the box and watched the rest of the races. I kept bugging him about Dillinger. I was fifteen at the time and wanted to report what we had been told to the authorities. Dad finally told me that he wouldn't take me to the races anymore if I believed everything I heard at the track.

That night we took the train home and Mom met us at the station. It was the Fourth of July. I told her about Dillinger hoping she would take my side against Dad, but she didn't. But Dad had gotten sick of me bugging him, and told me I could call up Hoover and tell him if I left Dad out of it. When we got home I called Hoover at his office and told him the story. And I told him that Dad didn't buy any part of it. He said that Dad was probably right but that I was a good citizen for reporting what I heard, and then he hung up.

We watched the fireworks at the Country Club that night, and the next day I played in a golf tournament. The sixteenth hole went right by our house and three men joined me on the tee and walked in with me. One was Dad, one was Hoover, and the other was Clyde Tolson, Hoover's assistant. They had dinner with us that night and then we drove Hoover and Tolson to the station. Dillinger was never mentioned. I asked Dad what Hoover had come to talk about, and Dad said something about "business," and changed the subject.

On Sunday July 22nd, I played golf again, and when I arrived home, Dad told me to take a shower and then turn on the radio and listen to the news. He said I might hear a story on Dillinger. I did what he said to do. About twenty minutes after I turned on the radio, a news flash came through. Dillinger had been shot and killed outside of the Biograph Theater on the south side of Chicago after attending the Sunday double feature. By the way, one of the movies was *Manhattan Melodrama*. It was produced by David O. Selznick, whom I mentioned earlier. Just a coincidence.

J. Edgar Hoover, his assistant, and Dad

But the story isn't over yet. A year and a half later I was attending Georgetown University in Washington D.C. FDR was President, and every year on his birthday he sponsored a Birthday Ball for the benefit of the March of Dimes. Dad always arranged for some movie stars to make appearances at the hotels and the theaters that participated. I was seventeen and got to escort Jean Harlow. I was living! At eleven p.m. we went to the White House where the President delivered a Fireside Chat and then thanked all the stars personally for attending.

That afternoon Dad had arranged for Hoover to take any of the stars who wanted to see it on a tour of the FBI. Jean wanted to go, and I got to take her. Jean got to fire a machine gun in the shooting range and seemed to get a kick out of it. I got a bigger kick out of the Dillinger exhibit. It contained, among other things, his death mask and the two guns he was carrying when he was killed. I remarked that I sure would like to have one of the guns, and Hoover said that so would a lot of other people. He quickly went on to the next exhibit.

Two or three days later an FBI agent knocked on the door of my room at Georgetown, and handed me a package. It contained one of Dillinger's guns, a thirty-eight in a forty-five frame. It was mounted in a case along with Hoover's business card. Written on the card, in Hoover's distinctive handwriting, was: "Dear Charlie, Here is the Dillinger gun you wanted. With my personal regards, J. Edgar Hoover."

I think I caught Dillinger. Do you?

CHAPTER 3

Trip to Europe

Mom, Benito Mussolini, and Dad

Graduation Present

I GRADUATED FROM GEORGETOWN
in 1939. I was 107th in a class of 108. We were
known as the cream of the college crop—rich and
thick. Dad took me to Europe as a graduation present.
He also took my best friend and golf partner, Johnny

Burke, with us. We sailed on an Italian cruise ship, the Saturnia. Dad had a photograph of himself, Mom and Mussolini taken in 1927. He casually left it out on the table for the steward to see. Our service was excellent.

We stopped at the Azores—Vigo, Spain—Lisbon, Portugal—Gibraltar—Morocco—and left the ship at Naples. We took the train to Rome—it ran on time—and checked into the Excelsior Hotel. Dad phoned Ambassador Phillips and got us invited to the Embassy for dinner. He then phoned a man named Enrico Galeazzi and said he'd like a private audience with the Pope. Galeazzi said that the Pope was not in the Vatican but was at his summer home, Castle Gondolfo. He also said he would pick us up at the hotel at nine the next morning and drive us out. Dad asked if he should call back and confirm the appointment, but Galeazzi said it would not be necessary. I'll tell you about Galeazzi later.

We went to the Embassy for dinner. Ambassador Phillips was an old Indiana buddy of Dad's, and they had fun swapping political stories. Phillip's secretary came in with a message, and Dad asked her if she would call Mussolini's office and make an appointment for us to see him tomorrow afternoon. She looked at Phillips for instructions. The Ambassador said, "He won't talk to Americans. He won't even talk to me." Dad said, "He'll talk to me. Do you want me to go through channels or call him personally?" Phillips told his secretary, "Oh hell, call him." Ten minutes later she came back. She seemed startled and puzzled, and looked back and forth from Phillips to Dad. Then she said, "The head of the government would like to see Mr. Pettijohn at 5:45 tomorrow afternoon." Phillips said, "Are you sure?" She said, "I think so." Dad said, "We can make it. We'll be back from Castle Gondolfo by then." I guess Phillips was impressed. He took us to the outdoor opera after dinner. We had good seats in a section reserved for diplomats.

Pope Pius XII

It was August 18, 1939. Galeazzi picked us up at nine and we drove twenty-five miles out on the Appian Way. Castle Gondolfo was at the top of a rise on a large estate. The main entrance was two large iron gates protected by four Swiss Guards wearing traditional medieval costumes and carrying lances. Galeazzi did not turn into the main gate. He kept going, and finally turned left on a dirt side road. He came to a small iron gate with only one Swiss Guard. The guard opened the gate when he saw the car and stood at attention while Galeazzi went through without stopping. We drove through the grounds and stopped in an archway at the side of the castle. There was an elevator in the archway. The door of the elevator was jammed open with a small block of wood. Galeazzi put the block of wood in his coat pocket, ushered us into the elevator and took us up two floors. We got out into a hallway and Galeazzi took the block of wood out of his pocket and jammed the door open. We walked down the hallway to another elevator, also jammed open with a block of wood.

Galeazzi took us up one more floor and did the block-of-wood-elevator-door business again. We were in the Pope's private apartments. Galeazzi showed us the Pope's bedroom and the small, private chapel where the Pope said Mass every morning. Galeazzi suggested that Johnny and I, being Catholics, might like to kneel and say a prayer in the Pope's chapel. He was right, and we did. He then looked at his watch and said it was time for our audience. He took us into a room about 60 feet by 20 feet and asked us to wait. He walked to the far end of the room and went out a door to his left.

Dad looked around the room. There was a riser behind us with a small, golden throne. Dad said, "That must be the Pope's throne. Why don't you sit on it? You can tell your mother about it." I said, "I don't think Mom would approve." Johnny said, "My mother would love it." He went up on the riser and sat on the throne for a second. If Johnny could, I could. I went up and sat down … just as the Pope came in the far door. I jumped awkwardly onto the floor, and I still don't know if he saw me or not. If he did, he never mentioned it. He was very courteous and spoke to us in perfect English. We knelt and kissed the Papal ring. Then he motioned for us to stand. I remember very little of the conversation, but he did ask us about Archbishop Spellman, who he had appointed to succeed Cardinal Hayes as Archbishop of New York. The Pope seemed pleased when we told him how much we admired Spellman. A few months later he made Spellman a Cardinal.

He knew that I had graduated from Georgetown, and said that he was happy that I had finally caught up with him. I was puzzled until he explained that he had gotten an honorary degree from Georgetown in 1938, when he had visited Washington as Papal Secretary of State.

Dad and Mom at the Vatican, 1940

After about ten minutes, Galeazzi indicated to us that it was time for the audience to end. Again, we knelt and kissed the Papal ring, and the Pope, master diplomat that he was, gave us the impression that he was disappointed that we had to leave. We retraced our steps to the car with Galeazzi doing the wood-block-elevator-door routine in reverse. Galeazzi drove back out through the side entrance. Again, the Swiss Guard spotted the car, and the gate was open when we reached it. That guard was the only person the four of us had seen on the Castle Gondolfo grounds other than the Pope himself.

Galeazzi drove us back to the hotel, and Dad asked him to have lunch with us. He said that he was very sorry but he had another appointment. Johnny and I were very curious about Galeazzi. How could a layman come and go as he pleased in the Pope's home and private quarters? I asked Dad how he knew him. Dad said he had never met him before, and that he was just a name and a phone number that Archbishop Spellman had given him.

I guess I better tell you about Enrico Galeazzi now. Archbishop Spellman explained him to me when Dad arranged for me to meet him a few months later. Spellman, as a young priest, had attended the Vatican College in Rome. One of his classmates, Eugenio Pacelli, the son of a wealthy Italian family, would become Pope Pius XII. Enrico Galeazzi was a young handyman working at the Vatican College. Young Father Pacelli was impressed with his honesty and diligence, and arranged for his family to put the boy through architectural school. He progressed rapidly and, by the time of our visit, had become the Papal Architect. He was also the Pope's closest friend. I guess that explains the wood-block-elevator door routine. By the way, Spellman told me something about Dad that I didn't know. It seems that the Pope wanted to see American newsreels in order to keep up with the political climate in the US, and Dad, at Spellman's request, had arranged for them to be delivered to the Vatican on a weekly basis. Maybe our audience was the Pope's courteous and gracious way of returning a small favor.

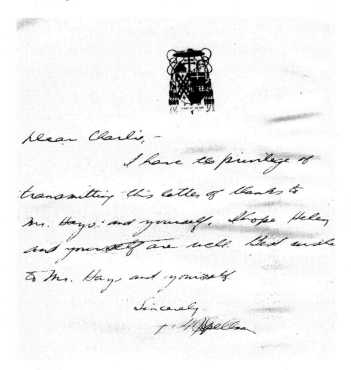

Cardinal Spellman's 1940 letter: "Dear Charlie, I have the privilege of transmitting this letter of thanks to Mr. Hays and yourself. I hope Helen and yourself are well. Best wishes to Mr. Hays and yourself. Sincerely, HG [His Grace] Spellman

DI SVA SANTITA

DAL VATICANO February 5, 1940.

N. 10610.

My dear Sir,

I am particularly pleased in accomplishing the venerated task of conveying to you the expression of the warm and paternal appreciation of His Holiness the Pope for the gift of a beautiful projection sound machine that has been offered by you to the Holy Father for His personal use.

His Holiness has deigned to accept your present, and He feels sure that the splendid machine might prove quite efficient and useful in giving to Him at times the very sight of the most important events of our days.

On this occasion the Holy Father asks you to convey his thanks also to Mr. Will H. Hays, who has cooperated with you so generously in securing the apparatus, and whom His Holiness ever remembers with deep interest and encouragement in the hard and most responsible task which he is confronted with.

Mr. Charles C. PETTIJOHN
General Counsel of the Motion Picture Producers
and Distributors of America, Inc.

NEW YORK

Furthermore, with most benevolent remembrance of your and your son's visit to Him last summer, the Holy Father from His heart imparts upon you and your devoted wife and family, as a pledge of special God's charity and favors, the Apostolic Benediction.

It is my pleasure to add my personal felicitation for such a special sign of august consideration, while I am happy to take this opportunity to remain

yours very sincerely in Christ

G.B. Montini

Pope Pius XII 1940 letter, written by G.B. Montini, later to become Pope Paul VI

Mussolini

It was still August 18, 1939. We caught a taxi in front of the hotel. Dad had told the doorman that we wanted to go to Mussolini's office. The doorman told the driver, and they both looked at us like we were crazy, but he took us to the gate. Dad gave his name to the security guard who passed us in immediately. The driver looked back at us again. His expression had changed. He didn't think we were crazy anymore. We stopped outside a rather flamboyant building entrance. Another security guard was waiting for us. He spoke English. He gave the taxi driver permission to wait for us, and then escorted us through several corridors and into Mussolini's office which seemed to me to be a mile long. Mussolini was seated at his desk at the far end. He was alone. The security guard left, and we started walking toward Mussolini. About halfway there Mussolini looked up and waved a greeting to Dad. Dad waved hello and then said, "I see you're parting your hair on the other side this year." Mussolini felt his bald head, broke into a smile and then laughed out loud. Johnny and I looked at each other. We were both glad he had a sense of humor. Dad introduced us, and he spoke to us in broken English. His son, Vittorio, had visited the US the previous year and had stayed overnight at our house. Dad had arranged for him to tour the Hollywood motion picture studios and talk to some producers, as Vittorio was setting up a motion picture studio in Rome.

Mussolini thanked Dad for taking care of his son, and then changed the subject to himself. He wanted to know what Americans thought of him as a government leader. Dad told him that Americans were impressed with the way he made the trains run on time, and added that our train from Naples to Rome was right on schedule. That wasn't exactly what Mussolini wanted to hear, but he did laugh politely. Then he buzzed for the security guard, bid us goodbye and we were escorted back to the taxi.

The driver treated us with great respect all the way back to the hotel. He spoke to the doorman in Italian who also suddenly started to treat us with great respect. That's about all that happened to us on August 18, 1939. I'm sure we had dinner someplace that night, but I forgot where it was.

Virginia Judd, Vittorio Mussolini, and Mom

Johnny Burke asked Dad how he got to know Mussolini, and Dad didn't know, but he told us the following story.

In 1927, the film industry had some money tied up in Italy and could not get it out of the country. Dad was sent to Europe to take a shot at getting the money out, and soon learned that Mussolini was the only person who could release it. Dad was unable to get an appointment with "Il Duce." Mom was with him on the trip and they proceeded on to Paris.

Dad had an old Indiana buddy named Tom Canty who worked for the State Department and was attached to our embassy in Paris. Dad and Mom took him to dinner and Dad mentioned his Mussolini problem. Canty said that he could have gotten Dad an appointment, and Dad said that if Canty wasn't kidding him he'd go back to Rome and see Mussolini. Canty told Dad to stop by the embassy the next day. Dad did so, and Canty handed him two sealed envelopes. He told Dad to give the first envelope to a man in Rome. The man's name and address were on the envelope. The other envelope had one word typed on it: "Mussolini." Canty told Dad to hand the second envelope directly to Mussolini before discussing business. He cautioned Dad against letting anyone else touch that envelope, emphasizing that it was for Mussolini's eyes only.

Dad went back to Rome, and the Mussolini appointment was arranged by the man whose name was on the first envelope. At ten o'clock the next day, Dad went to Mussolini's office for his appointment. He took Mom with him. Per instructions, he handed Mussolini the envelope. Mussolini glared at him but he opened the envelope and took out a folded piece of paper. He unfolded the paper, and a butterfly made out of tissue paper and wire, which had been wrapped in a tightened rubber band, was propelled into Il Duce's face. It made somewhat of a racket. Dad and Mom were terrified and came close to relieving themselves on the spot. The Dictator pointed his finger in Dad's face, glowered, and looked him in the eye. He said two words: "Tom Canty." Then he burst out laughing, saying "ho ho ho" several times in Italian. The tension was broken. They talked business and Mussolini released the money. He was still "ho ho ho-ing" when Mom and Dad left.

They rushed back to Paris and Dad went to the embassy to thank Tom Canty. Unfortunately, Tom had died the night before of a heart attack. That's why Dad didn't know how he got to meet Mussolini. He never found out about the butterfly, either.

Cannes, Joe Kennedy And My Pal Eddie

The next day we took the train from Rome to Cannes on the French Riviera. The train left on time. We stayed at the Martinez, right on the beach. Joseph P. Kennedy, the United States Ambassador to England, was also there on vacation. He was another old friend of Dad's and arranged for Johnny and me to play golf on a local course. We played a twosome and had an enjoyable round until we got to the fifteenth hole, where we caught up with a foursome. They were very slow and did not offer to let us play through. The fifteenth was a par three, and while we waited on the tee, a golfer playing by himself caught up with us. He asked, "I say, won't they let you play through?" I told him that they didn't offer to, and asked if he would like to play the last four holes with us. He said, "That's very nice of you. I'd appreciate it." I introduced myself, telling him my name was Charlie

Pettijohn and my partner was Johnny Burke. He shook hands with both of us and gave his name as Eddie Windsor. We played the last four holes together and he thanked us, excused himself, and left. It seemed he had an appointment and didn't have time to stop in the clubhouse for a drink.

When we got back to the Martinez, we thanked Ambassador Kennedy and told him about the round. He looked at us in amazement, and asked us if we didn't realize that we had played the last four holes with the former King Edward VIII of Great Britain. Johnny said, "I thought he seemed familiar, but I couldn't quite place him." I said, "Why did he introduce himself as Eddie Windsor when his real name is David Windsor?" The Ambassador said, "Well, I guess he was just putting you on." Come to think of it, I guess he was right.

Cannes To Paris To London

The next morning at breakfast Dad told us that our plans had changed. We had to leave Cannes a few days early, and we took a train to Paris. We stayed at the Georges Cinq[1] for two days. Dad made arrangements for us to play golf at St. Cloud. Once again we played a twosome, and our caddy was an elderly French lady who carried both our bags and wore wooden shoes. On one hole I asked her what club to use for my second shot. She said *cinq*. I thought she meant that I should go back

---

1 The hotel is now called the "Four Seasons Hotel George V."

to the hotel. Johnny, who had taken French in school, explained that *cinq* meant "five." I hit the shot with a five iron about five feet from the pin. The elderly lady was right—I made my five foot putt for a birdie *trois*. Remembering Cannes, Johnny and I looked carefully around the course for celebrities. We didn't see any, or if we did, once again, we didn't recognize them.

Back at the hotel, Dad told us we were leaving for London the next morning. He indicated that war was imminent, and we should get home as soon as possible. We flew to London and stayed at the Savoy Hotel. Ambassador Kennedy, who had returned from Cannes, came by the hotel to talk to Dad. Once again he arranged for us to play golf. He also helped Dad switch our return reservations from the *Queen Mary* to the *Normandie*. Johnny and I played golf at a course called Addington, and we enjoyed it very much. Once again we kept our eye out for celebrities, but we came up empty. Apparently George VI had more important things to do at the time than play golf.

The Last Trip Of The Normandie

We took the train to Southampton and boarded the *Normandie*. It was the end of August. Originally, Dad had planned for us to return a week later on the *Queen Mary*.

The passenger list was quite interesting, and I got to meet them all. I remember Harry Cohn, the President of Columbia Pictures, as well as actor Roland Young, who told me how much he enjoyed making *Topper*. Sonja

Henie, the Olympic ice skater, was also a passenger. I remember Johnny made a semi-amorous suggestion to her, but her mother cut Johnny off. James Stewart was also on the *Normandie*, and we played a couple of games of ping pong. About three days out at sea, Dad tried sending a wire to Mother, and was informed that the Captain had blacked out all radio transmissions. It also happened to other passengers, and word spread around the ship that war had been declared. The ship was suddenly blacked out, but the passengers got no information. We arrived in New York two days later and learned that war had not been declared.

The *Normandie* docked at its usual berth at the 88th Street Pier. Mom met us and took us home. A few days later, September 3, 1939, war was declared in Europe. The *Queen Mary* was also blacked out, but completed her trip. War had been declared in the middle of her voyage. The *Normandie* never left the dock again. A month later, she caught fire and sank. The *Queen Mary* got out later, and became a "troopship."

CHAPTER 4

Politics

Winsted, New York

I STILL REMEMBER OUR phone number at Winsted. It was a good old party line shared by eight or ten other cottages on the lake. You were just supposed to answer the phone if the operator rang your code, and ours was one long ring and three short ones. I don't think anyone stuck to this rule ... everybody always picked up the phone and listened anyway, just to find out what their neighbors were doing.

One summer in 1935, I answered our ring. It was Senator Huey P. Long calling Dad. I asked the Senator to hold on a minute 'cause Dad was sitting on our neighbor's dock next door. I just missed Dad as our neighbor's wife had been listening on the party line and had gotten to him first. He took Huey Long's call on the neighbor's phone. I didn't know at the time what Huey and Dad talked about, but the other neighbors did, and they came over later in the day to discuss the call with Dad.

Quite a while later, Dad told me that Huey had gotten mad at his coverage on one of the newsreels, and had established a State of Louisiana Motion Picture Censor Board, and that no films could be exhibited in Louisiana until they had been approved by the Censor Board for a substantial fee. Dad finally talked Huey into dissolving the Censor Board, but the Senator was assassinated before he had a chance to do it. It took Dad almost a year to get the law establishing the Censor Board repealed.

Some Political Stuff About Herbert Hoover, Al Smith and FDR

As a lobbyist, Dad was always involved in politics. His job was to figure out which candidate was going to win, and then contribute motion picture money to the winning candidate's campaign fund. He never missed.

The first thing I can remember about politics happened in 1928. I was nine years old. My brother, Bruce, and I went to Rye Country Day School. It was an expensive school for rich men's kids. Westchester County was full of rich men. They were all Republicans. To teach the students the importance of voting, the school held a mock election. Bruce and I were Catholics. Mom was a Catholic. She loved Al Smith[1] and wanted us to vote for him. Dad was smart. He kept out of the discussions. Bruce and I voted for

1 Al Smith was the opposing Democratic presidential candidate to Herbert Hoover in 1928. Before running for President, Smith was the governor of New York for four terms. Smith was the first Roman Catholic presidential candidate, which resulted in an increased

Smith. The final tally at Rye Country Day School was 96 to 2 in favor of Herbert Hoover. When it became known that Bruce and I were the two who voted for Smith, some of the parents wouldn't let their children play with us anymore.

In 1932, Dad took us to the Democratic Convention in Chicago. Al Smith and FDR were the favorites for the nomination for President. Dad knew in advance that FDR would win, and exerted his efforts in FDR's favor. Mom and I were still for Al Smith, and she bought me a Smith campaign button, which I wore proudly. At the convention, Al Smith's name was placed in the nomination first. All of his delegates paraded around the floor waving banners. Mom and I jumped up and applauded and cheered.

After the demonstration died down, Roosevelt's name was placed in nomination. His delegates paraded and cheered and made a lot more noise than the Smith demonstrators. I started to cry, and Dad took me up the ramp to buy me a hot dog. Will Rogers was standing at the hot dog stand, and Dad introduced me to him. He was wearing an Al Smith button, too. He looked down the ramp where Roosevelt supporters were parading. Then he turned to me, looked at my button, and then looked at his button. "Son," he said, "I guess we're the only two left."

---

amount of voters in the '28 elections. The election ended in a landslide with Hoover winning with an overwhelming majority.

The Roosevelt Party
Oregon – California
Line
September 23, 1932.

*FDR's 1932 Presidential Campaign: Dad on train plat-
form and Joe Kennedy fifth from left, front row.*

Maybe you'd like to know why Dad never missed the outcome of an election. Back in the twenties and thirties, before television, everybody went to the movies. There was always a newsreel, and the newsreels always showed clips of the candidates making speeches. The theater audience would applaud when their favorite candidate appeared. Dad had theater managers all over the country report to him the name of the candidate who got the most applause in their theater. Like I said, he never missed.

Jim Farley

I think it was 1936, and Dad was in Washington D.C. staying at the Mayflower Hotel. He took me out to dinner and when we came back to the hotel, Jim Farley, Chairman of the Democratic Party and Postmaster General, was sitting in the lobby. He and Dad were old friends from the Roosevelt campaigns. Farley called to Dad, and we went over to his chair. I had never met Farley, and Dad introduced me to him. We shook hands, and then he talked business with Dad. Then Dad and I went up to our room. I think that they had only talked for two or three minutes. Two years later, Dad was in town again, and I went to the Mayflower to see him. I was walking through the lobby by myself when I saw Farley in his chair. He saw me at the same time and called, "Hey, Charlie, is your father in town?" I said, "Yes, Mr. Farley, he's up in his room." He said, "Tell him I'd like to talk to him." I said, "Yes, Mr. Farley." I did what I was told. I had heard many stories about Jim Farley's memory. Many people claimed that Farley never forgot a name or a face. He sure proved it to me that day.

FDR

I think it was January, 1937. Dad had come down to Washington to arrange the President's Birthday Ball. He was staying at the Mayflower Hotel, and I came down from Georgetown to have lunch with him. He put my lunch on his expense account. It tasted better than the food we had at school. This time he got a call from

David Selznick, who was about to produce *Gone with the Wind*. The call was something about who was going to play Scarlett O'Hara. After Dad hung up, I asked him who was going to play Scarlett O'Hara. Dad said David hadn't told him.

Among the guests gathered around First Lady Eleanor Roosevelt at FDR's 1940 Birthday Ball are Red Skelton, Mickey Rooney, Edward G. Robinson, and James Cagney

President Roosevelt always did a coast to coast "Fireside Chat" the night they had the Birthday Ball. I had an idea. It was unusual for a rich man's kid. I said, "Dad, why don't you ask Selznick who's going to play Scarlett O'Hara? Maybe the President will announce it during his fireside chat tonight." Dad thought a moment, then called Selznick back, handed me the phone and said, "Tell David." I did. David asked me to hang on and wait. I waited twenty minutes before he came back on the phone. He told me it was a good idea but that he wasn't ready to make the announcement yet. I asked him if he'd tell me, and he said, "No." That night, all the Hollywood stars went to the White House for the Fireside Chat. I was Janet Gaynor's escort. After the chat I told the President about my conversation with Selznick. He said he would have been very happy to make the announcement, and then asked me if I knew who was going to play Scarlett O'Hara. I told him that Selznick wouldn't tell me, either.

* * *

One of my classmates at Georgetown was Francis Yockey. He thought he was an authority on everything, and talked all the time. He told impossible stories that none of our classmates believed.

One day Dad was in town and was staying at the Willard Hotel, a block and a half from the White House. I went down to the hotel for one of Dad's expense account lunches, and I took Yockey with me. When we finished eating, Dad decided we should go for a walk. As we passed the White House, Dad noticed the American Flag flying over the Executive Office Building. He told us that FDR was in his office at the time because the flag was only flown while the President was actually in the Oval Office. Yockey thought Dad was wrong about that, so Dad said, "Let's find out." We walked through the White House gate, the guard waved at us and said, "Hello, Mr. Pettijohn" to Dad. We walked up to the Executive Office Building where another man walked out the door to greet us. Dad introduced him to us as Colonel Starling, the head of the Secret Service Agents who guarded the President. Dad asked him if the "Boss" was busy. Starling said he didn't know, but that Dad should go ask "Mac." "Mac" was Marvin MacIntyre, FDR's Appointment Secretary. His office adjoined the Oval Office. Mac greeted Dad warmly, and Dad introduced us to him. Mac told us to sit down. He said the "Boss" was in a meeting that should break up in a few minutes.

FDR

About five minutes later, a buzzer buzzed, and Mac got up and opened the door to the Oval Office. He said, "Mr. President, an old friend just dropped by." The President said, "Who is it?" Mac said, "Charlie Pettijohn." The

President called, "Come on in, Charlie." Dad got up and walked in, motioning us to follow. Roosevelt remembered me, called me by name, and motioned me over to shake hands. I did as I was told, and Yockey followed me to Roosevelt's desk. I introduced him, and he shook Yockey's hand, too. Then he told us he wanted to talk to Dad for a few minutes, and Yockey and I went back to Mac's office. Dad came out about ten minutes later and we continued our walk. Yockey was dumbfounded and never said a word.

When we got back to Georgetown, he told all the other students that he had met the President. Because of his "tall story" reputation, nobody believed him. Then he asked me to back his story, and for the hell of it, I never did.

Guess Who Came to Dad's House for Dinner

Joe and Rose Kennedy lived in Bronxville, New York, and the Kennedys and the Pettijohns often visited each other. One day, the Kennedys arrived at our house. The children were sent out in the yard to play. Jack Kennedy found the strawberry patch, and we all sat on the ground and ate all the strawberries. Jack ate most of them. George, the gardener, saw what we did. All the strawberries were gone, and George got mad and told Mother. Rose Kennedy heard what George said, and called Jack in the house and spanked him. Mother was the perfect hostess. She called me in the house and spanked me. I didn't think that was fair … I really didn't like strawberries very much.

Jack didn't exactly disappear into obscurity. Some thirty-five years later he reappeared as President of the United States.

* * *

R.E. Peters, Clarence Darrow, Arthur Mullin, and Dad, 1932

Many other people came to the house, and I got to meet them. I remember Mayor Jimmie Walker, who talked about building the New York subways. James Cagney came to the house once. He was having an argument with Warner Brothers over his contract. Dad stepped in and settled the argument. Cagney was very grateful to Dad ... so were the Warner Brothers. Clarence Darrow and his wife, Ruby, stayed overnight once. He had been booked into a debate at the County Center in White Plains, New York.

And I got to hear the debate. Clarence Darrow won. I don't remember whom he debated, but it didn't make any difference. Darrow would have won anyway.

* * *

Once, Howard Hughes came to the house. He had to meet a Broadway actress who was coming down on the train from Boston. He was supposed to meet her at Greenwich, Connecticut. He didn't know where Greenwich was, so I went in his car with him to show him. You may have heard of her. Later she became a movie star. The girl was named Ginger Rogers.

* * *

Some people collected coins, other people collected stamps. My mother collected priests. She always invited them to dinner. She even bought them highball glasses with their names engraved on them. One day, Dad bought a glass for himself. He had "The Protestant" engraved on it. Dad's glass was only half as big as the priests' glasses.

Every year Notre Dame played Army at Yankee Stadium. The team stayed at the Westchester Country Club, and practiced on the polo field. On Friday nights before the game, Knute Rockne[2] always came to our house. So did a lot of the Notre Dame "Subway Alumni"

---

2 Knute Rockne is one of the most famous collegiate football coaches in history and coached Notre Dame's football team to victory from 1918 to 1930. His record for winning seasons is still the highest in both collegiate and professional football statistics.

[fans of Notre Dame sports who did not actually attend Notre Dame]. Once I got to meet "The Four Horsemen" who were famous members of the Notre Dame football team during Rockne's reign. They had graduated, but they always showed up for the Army game. Of course, all of Mom's priests were also in attendance.

Everyone was Catholic and, therefore, could not eat meat on Friday. But "The Protestant" could. So, Dad bought a small ham for himself. One time, Rockne saw Dad's ham, waited until midnight, and asked Dad for a sandwich. So did all the alumni and all the priests. Dad had to cut the ham into very, very small, thin pieces. Rockne claimed that there was no ham in the sandwich. Dad said, "Knute, the ham was there...you just bit beyond it." The other guests heard what Dad said and took smaller bites. The ham was there.

Rockne was very nice to me and let me ride into Yankee Stadium with the players and sit on the bench during the game. I also got to go into the locker room at half-time and listen to Rockne make several of his famous half-time speeches. If I were smart I would have made some notes. But being a dumb kid, I didn't.

* * *

Once, there was a party for Morton Downey, the Irish tenor, who had just married Barbara Bennett, Constance's and Joan's sister. Richard Bennett, her father, was there, too. So were all of Mother's priests and a lot of our neighbors. Dad liked to mix the drinks himself. He had his own cooler which held club soda and ginger ale. Tom Taggert, who owned French Lick Springs, a health resort in Indiana, had sent Dad a couple of cases of Pluto Water. It was a mineral water that was a sure cure for people suffering from constipation. By mistake, Dad used it as a drink mix. He thought it was plain soda. After a while, some of our guests started to disappear. We had seven bathrooms in our house and, before long, all of them were occupied. The other guests were lined up outside the bathroom doors waiting their turn.

His Royal Highness, the Crown Prince, Fumitaka Konoye, JFK And Old Parr

I met Fumitaka Konoye, who went to Lawrenceville Prep School, at the Interscholastic Gold Championships in Greenwich, Connecticut, in 1934. His father, at the time Premier of Japan, was visiting this country and attended the golf tournament. Fumi introduced me to him, and I remember calling him, "King." I thought that all Princes' fathers were Kings, but Fumi pointed out that I was wrong. His father was not a King, but a Prince, too.

Anyway, Fumi and I became friends, and played in several other golf tournaments. He then went to Princeton and played on the Princeton Golf Team. I went to Georgetown and played on the Georgetown Golf Team.

In 1937 or 1938, I forget which, Princeton and Harvard came to Georgetown to play a round-robin. The Japanese

Embassy gave a big party for all the golfers. Jack Kennedy, although not a golfer, had come down from Harvard.

Having known Jack since we were kids, we had a drink together at the party. The Embassy was serving a scotch called Old Parr which we had never heard of, but it was the best scotch we had ever tasted. We mentioned this to Fumi, and for the next two years at Georgetown, a bottle of Old Parr was always in my locker at the golf club. The Japanese Embassy did good work.

More than twenty years went by, and I was living in North Hollywood, California. The Democratic National Convention was in Los Angeles and Jack Kennedy was nominated for President. This was 1960. I watched his acceptance speech on television, and about an hour later my phone rang. It was Jack Kennedy. I offered congratulations, and then he asked me the name of the scotch that we had enjoyed at the Japanese Embassy more than twenty years before. I told him it was Old Parr, and he wanted to know where to get it. I told him I had looked for it, but had never been able to find any. I was surprised that Joe Kennedy's son would ask me where to find whiskey, and suggested that when he became President he would probably have no trouble finding Old Parr. I asked him to send me a case when he found it, and he said he would do so. That was the last time I ever talked to Jack Kennedy. I never got the scotch, but I am sure he would have sent me a case if he had found it.

CHAPTER 5

Sports

Me and a baseball teammate

Mel Ott and the End of My Baseball Career

PROBABLY BECAUSE OF Uncle Jimmy and
Mom's catcher's mitt, I pitched for the Rye
Country Day School team when I was in the

seventh and eighth grades. I had a pretty good record, except for the time that Dad hit the home run over the Boston Post Road. At Portsmouth Priory, I pitched a couple of games for their freshman team. My last three years at Georgetown, I played golf instead of baseball.

In 1939, two of the Georgetown regulars, Joe Keegan and Harry Bassin, were asked to try out with the New York Giants at the Polo Grounds after their graduation. They stayed at our house in Rye, and I drove them in to the Polo Grounds every morning so they could work out with the Giants. Mel Ott was the manager, and someone told him I used to be a pitcher. He asked me to pitch batting practice and I did so. He told me I looked pretty good and asked me to come back the next day. I did so, and again pitched batting practice. Again, he told me I looked pretty good and asked me back the next day. Pitching batting practice wasn't easy, and my arm got tired. Also, the hitters seemed intent on killing me by hitting line drives right at me. After the third day, I went to Ott and demanded a contract. With great tact and diplomacy, Ott said, "Get out of here, you bum. Don't you know I've been putting you on for three days?" Being a dumb kid, I was unable to figure it out, but I knew my major league career was over before it started. Joe and Harry didn't make it either, and they were *good* ball players.

The Golden Years Of Sports

I guess for an eight- to ten-year-old sports fan whose mother owned her own catcher's glove, the twenties was the decade to grow up in. I told you about Babe Ruth. Now I'll tell you about Jack Dempsey, Gene Tunney, and Walter Hagen.

Billy Gibson, who managed Gene Tunney, lived two houses down the road from us. I went to school with his kids. Several times he brought Tunney by for a visit while getting him ready to fight Jack Dempsey for the title. Mom and Dad knew Dempsey, too, although I never met him as a kid. Mom liked Dempsey the best, and the night of the title fight in Chicago in 1927, we went into the living room to listen to it on the radio. In those days, we used to look at the radio while listening to it. Come to think of it, I guess that's why Lee De Forest invented the television tube. He probably figured that if people were gonna sit around looking at radios, they might as well see pictures, too. But to get back to the fight, Tunney knocked Dempsey out after the celebrated "long count." Mom cried.

When I was fifteen, I got to play golf with the great Walter Hagen. He had come to the Westchester Country Club to play an exhibition match to raise money for charity. I was club champion then, and got to fill out the foursome, along with Lou Costello, the club professional, and Archie Compson, an English professional. Hagen had been up very late the night before, and was somewhat shaky on the first tee. But on the first hole he ended up with a ten foot putt for a birdie. Just as he was about to putt, a small dog ran across the green between his legs. Hagen never flinched and knocked his putt right in the back of the cup. On the next tee, I asked him if the dog that ran between his legs had bothered him.

He look at me with a quizzical expression and asked, "Son, was that a real dog?"

The 1934 All Star Game

Another of Dad's friends was Judge Kenesaw Mountain Landis, the "Czar" of baseball. In 1934, he invited Dad and me to sit in his box at the All-Star game in the Polo Grounds [in New York City]. This was the game in which Carl Hubbell struck out five sluggers in a row. They were Babe Ruth, Lou Gehrig, Jimmie Foxx, Al Simmons, and Joe Cronin, in the first and second innings. No one mentions the other four American League starters. I still remember who they were and what they did.

Goose Goslin was the first man up and he singled. Hubbell then walked Charlie Gehringer. Hubbell then proceeded to strike out the famous five consecutively. Then Bill Dickey singled. The next hitter was Lefty Gomez, and Hubbell struck him out to end the inning. I don't remember much about the rest of the game, but the American League finally won 9 to 7. It sure wasn't Hubbell's fault.

My Second And Third Holes- In- One

On July 15, 1935, the *New York Sun* called me a "Golf Prodigy." I was sixteen years old at the time. I started playing golf at the age of four, and by the age of ten scored my first hole-in-one on the number four hole at the Westchester-Biltmore Country Club.

Hole-in-One

C. C. PETTIJOHN, JR.

Attention of golfers at the Westchester Biltmore was centered this week on Charles C. Pettijohn, son of Mr. and Mrs. Pettijohn of Manhattan avenue, Biltmore grounds, who has the distinction of making the fourth hole on the Biltmore course in one stroke.

Me, the Golf Prodigy

In 1937, Johnny Burke and I flew out to Portland, Oregon, to play in the National Amateur. I qualified for match play but got beaten in the first round. Johnny missed qualifying. We then flew down to Los Angeles to play in the Western Amateur, at the Los Angeles Country Club. During a practice round, Johnny and I teamed up against Frank Strafaci and Joe Thompson. We were playing for a hell of a lot of Dad's money. We were all even when we got to the last hole. It was a hundred and sixty yard, par three ... we had played the last nine first. Frank and Joe teed off first and knocked their shots about ten feet from the hole. Johnny knocked his in the trap. I think at this point if my Fairy Godmother had ever given me a golf ball that would go in the hole the first time I hit it, I would have saved it for this particular situation. So I teed up my ball, hit it with a five iron, and the damn thing hit the green and rolled into the cup. Frank and Joe started tearing up twenty-dollar bills and throwing them at me. Francis Ouimet, the grand old man of golf, had been playing just ahead of us. After holing out, he stood behind the green to watch us hit our shots. He knew we had some big bets. He waited for me to come to the green, and came over and shook my hand. He said he had been playing golf for many years and had never had a hole-in-one. And that this was the first one he'd ever seen.

I missed qualifying for the Western Amateur, but Johnny qualified and went to the semi-finals. Then we went back to New York.

My third hole-in-one, and apparently my last one, came in 1948. It was on the sixth hole at Lakeside Golf Club in Toluca Lake. I was playing a threesome with Stan Jones and Jimmy Leicester. The hole was ninety yards long, and I hit it with a wedge. It hit the back of the green, bounced over and disappeared from sight just for an instant. Then the back-spin took, the ball came back on the green and rolled into the cup. Jimmy had turned away when the ball had disappeared over the green … he didn't see the ball go in the hole. But I saw it, and Stan saw it, and the caddies saw it. Jimmy refused to believe it. I made him go over to the cup and take my ball out. He thought we planted the ball in the cup to play a trick on him. At Lakeside, when you make a hole-in-one, you have to buy a drink for all the members in the bar. Jimmy wouldn't even accept his drink.

How To Get Married Without Missing A Golf Tournament

Josephine Ursula Hanlon lived in New Rochelle. She was the youngest of four children, and her family called her "Sis." Everybody called her "Sis." I did, too. That's why I have gone through life calling my wife, "Sis." We went together through the last two years I was in college and always planned to be married. Or maybe Dad and Mom planned it. They liked "Sis" better than they liked me. And, as always, they were right.

After I graduated from Georgetown, we had to wait fifteen months before we could get married. It was Dad's fault. He had an old fashioned idea that his son should get a job before he got a wife. I wasn't easy to employ. It took him fifteen months to get me a job. But he and Will Hayes finally talked Joe Breen into giving me a job as an editor on the Motion Picture Production Code Board.

The job came through rather suddenly. I was in Newport, Rhode Island, playing in a golf tournament. On a Wednesday night, Dad phoned me at Johnny Burke's house. He told me to come home...that I was getting married Monday. I told him that the tournament did not end until Sunday. I could come home Monday if he could make the wedding Tuesday. He told me to call Sis and arrange it. I told him to call Sis...he could arrange things better than I could. He did, and talked her into it.

She didn't have a wedding dress, but she had a friend her size who was getting married a week later. She talked her friend into giving her the dress, and they both went to Altman's so her friend could have another fitting. The dress fit Sis perfectly.

I came home Monday and we got married Tuesday morning at ten o'clock. We were married by Father John J. Kehoe, S.J., who was the Dean of Discipline at Georgetown University and had personally suspended me from school three times during my college career. Dad was always able to get me reinstated. I'm sure the infractions were very minor.

The honeymoon was also a minor problem. Johnny and I had another golf tournament to play in at Winged Foot on Friday. After the wedding reception, Sis and I drove up to the cottage at Winsted, Connecticut. Johnny Burke and Sis's sister, Ruth, followed about an hour behind us. Johnny's brother, Joe, and his wife drove down from Newport to Winsted and met us at the cottage. The six of us had a lovely honeymoon.

We drove to Rye Thursday night and played in the golf tournament Friday, Saturday, and Sunday. There was another minor problem. Dad and Mom had wanted us to take the train to the coast with them on Wednesday, but that would have ruined the golf tournament. Instead, they took our baggage with them on the train, and we flew out Sunday night after the tournament.

Sis and me at our wedding

A Note From Adrienne: After Mom and Dad Got Married In 1940

Mom and Dad moved from New York to Hollywood, California, where his father bought him a house in a neighborhood known as Toluca Lake. Grandpa's friend, David Selznick, had recommended Toluca Lake simply because it was north of Hollywood, and Dad wouldn't have to drive into the sun during his commute to work, which would be the case if Dad moved to Beverly Hills where the Selznicks lived.

PART 2

Adventures in California

CHAPTER 6

Toluca Lake

An Introduction by Adrienne

LOTS OF PEOPLE in the entertainment business lived in Toluca Lake: the Disney family, the Bob Hope family, Ron Howard, Tex Ritter, Cher, the Kerns Preserves & Jellies family, Ann Blythe, Frank Sinatra's nieces and nephews, the Aaron Brothers family, Lassie, Bireley's Orange Soda family, Jonathan Winters, Julie Andrews, and countless writers, producers, directors, and music composers.

Toluca Lake was located at the base of the hills which divided downtown Hollywood from North Hollywood. It was a small neighborhood, and because everyone worked together, everyone knew one another. And everyone's kids played together and went to the local schools. Warner Brothers film studios bordered Toluca Lake. The boys in the neighborhood used to ride their bikes over to the WB lot and play on the western street set. One day, they were caught by the security guard and assembled in the security office. The guard knew my Dad because they were umpires on the neighborhood Little League Team, so he called Dad to come get the boys. Dad was watching a golf game on

TV and asked his friend to keep the boys "secure" until the game was over. No problem. According to my brother's version of the story, the boys remained huddled in the security office, terrified of what was going to happen to them, until Dad came to get them. I'm not sure if they ever played on the WB lot again, but if they did, they definitely were not caught again!

* * *

Every Thursday night some of the men in the neighborhood played in a poker game. Tex Ritter, the country western star, was one of them. He lived around the corner from us, and our kids played together. My youngest daughter, Adrienne, used to play with Tex's son, Jonathan. They were both dramatically inclined and put on plays together in the garage. Naturally, Tex and I had to watch them. The plays always had the same theme… Jonathan was the monster, complete with pratfalls and strange faces, and Adrienne was the heartbroken lady-in-distress. We had seen better plays, but of course we didn't tell the kids that. They were only eight or nine years old at the time. A couple of years later, the Ritters moved away. And Adrienne was truly heartbroken when she lost touch with Jonathan. About fifteen years later, they ran into each other at CBS Television City. Jonathan, now known as John, was the star of the TV series, *Three's Company*, complete with pratfalls and strange faces. Adrienne had become a TV Associate Director and was working on *The Young and The Restless*. Adrienne was overjoyed and wanted to take up where she and Jonathan had left off. John was very courteous, but pointed out that he was already married. Once again, Jonathan was the monster and Adrienne was the brokenhearted lady-in-distress. Come to think of it, both the kids were doing very well. Maybe Tex and I were wrong about those "dumb" plays in the garage.

* * *

Kristie Stone lived next door to us. She was the same age as my daughter, Muffy, and they used to play together. Kristie had another girlfriend with an unpronounceable Armenian name. One day Kristie and the Armenian girl were playing in our yard. I don't know where Muffy was. I was taking a nap, and they put the garden hose through my bedroom window and squirted me. I rushed into the yard and kicked the Armenian girl in her fanny. Kristie jumped over the wall and got away. I'd forgotten the incident until years later when I ran into the Armenian girl at CBS Television City. She had not forgotten the incident, and called it to my attention. She had also changed her name, and was starring with her husband in *The Sonny and Cher Show*.

* * *

Kay and Gretchen Diebel used to babysit for us when my daughters, Muffy and Adrienne, were growing up. They were very trustworthy, and my wife, Sis, and I were good friends with their parents. When they came of age, Gretchen married Duke Wayne's son Michael and had five children. Kay married Frankie Avalon and had nine chilren. Adrienne and Muffy were kept very busy babysitting for their babysitters' children.

* * *

Two more of our neighbors were Ray and Nina Sebastian. Ray was a makeup man for motion pictures. One day Sis got a phone call from a man who knew we were close friends of the Sebastians. He was giving a party for Ray's birthday and wanted us to come to his house for dinner, but we shouldn't tell Ray because it was a surprise party. Sis asked him who he was, and he said he was Tyrone Power. Sis was skeptical and said, "Sure, and I'm Greta Garbo." Tyrone finally convinced her that he was really him, and gave her an address and a phone number. We went to his house with two other neighbors, John and Dorothy McKean, and the "surprise party" worked. Tyrone Power was very friendly and hospitable and so was his girlfriend, Mai Zetterling, who was a very gracious hostess. Ray Sebastian was not only Tyrone's makeup man, but also one of his closest friends. A few years later, when Tyrone died in Spain, he died in Ray Sebastian's arms.

CHAPTER 7

Lakeside Stories

Lakeside Golf Club

An Introduction by Adrienne

LAKESIDE GOLF CLUB *was located in Toluca Lake. It was founded in 1924 and because of its proximity to the studios, the majority of its members were from the entertainment industry. And most of them lived in Toluca Lake.*

* * *

I joined the Lakeside Golf Club in 1941. The Lakeside members, for the most part, were connected with the motion picture industry. They included Bing Crosby, Bob Hope—a golf partner of mine from back east who proposed me for membership—W.C. Fields, Howard Hughes and, from only two blocks away at Warner Brothers, Humphrey Bogart, Erroll Flynn, Dennis Morgan, Jack Carson and, once in a while, Ann Sheridan. Anyway, here are some Lakeside stories.

Rudy Ralston

Herbert J. Yates owned Republic Studios which produced all the Gene Autry and Roy Rogers pictures, along with many others. Mr. Yates belonged to Lakeside and loved to play golf. He married Vera Hrubá Ralston, the ice skater, and made several pictures with her. He also "inherited" her brother, Rudy, who joined Lakeside so he could play golf with Mr. Yates. Rudy wanted to become a producer, and he finally figured out how to get there. Every time Mr. Yates had a three or four foot putt, Rudy would say, "That's good, Mr. Yates," and pick up his ball and hand it to him. His plan worked perfectly, and Mr. Yates soon made Rudy a producer.

Barbara Stanwyck

While I was working at Universal, Barbara Stanwyck arrived a few minutes late for a story conference on an upcoming property. She apologized for her tardiness, but explained that she had been delayed at a filling station.

It seems that the attendant was busy servicing another car for two somewhat elderly ladies. Barbara had gotten out to clean her own windshield when one of the ladies called her over and asked her if she was a movie star. Barbara told them that she had made a number of pictures, and then the other old lady asked if she was Mary Pickford. Rather than spoil their day, Barbara told them she was Mary Pickford and let it go at that.

Buddy Rogers, also a Lakeside member and Mary's husband, used to bring her over to Lakeside for dinner every once in a while. They came in one night about a week after the Barbara Stanwyck meeting, and I told the story to Mary. Mary laughed and said to tell Barbara that she did absolutely right. Mary promised that for the sake of the little old ladies she would never make another picture ... Barbara's secret was safe with her.

Barbara Stanwyck (left) and Mary Pickford (right) c.1940s
[Corbis Images]

Bob Hope and Del Webb

On October 8, 1956, we were sitting in the Lakeside bar watching the last game of the Yankees / Dodgers World Series. It was the eighth inning, and Don Larsen was pitching a perfect game. Bob Hope suddenly got an idea. He was preparing a show for the next week and said he'd sure like to have Don Larsen appear on it if he pitched a perfect game. Del Webb, another Lakeside member, owned the Yankees at the time, and Bob said, "I wonder how I can get hold of Del and see if he could get Don to do the show." Another Lakeside member who was watching the game with us told Bob to call Yankee Stadium and the switchboard could connect him to Del, who had a phone in his box. Bob did so, and he was connected with Del, who said he'd talk to Larsen if he pitched a perfect game. Don did, and Del did, and Bob had the perfect game pitcher on his show. After Bob had completed his call, he turned to the member who had told him how to reach Del. He asked, "How did you know Del had a phone in his box?" The member was Don Ameche. You may remember the movie in which he played Alexander Graham Bell.

Bing Crosby's House Burned Down

I remember one Christmas season when I was at the bar at Lakeside. The phone rang and I answered it. It was Dixie Crosby trying to find Bing. Their house was on fire. He wasn't at Lakeside, but I thought he was at a bar (nearby) on Ventura Boulevard. I called the bar ... it was a good guess. Bing was there. I told him his house was on fire, and he rushed home. I drove over to see if I could be of any help. But it was too late. I sat on the stone wall with Dixie and the kids, and watched the firemen do the best they could. I was sitting next to the twins when they got in an argument. It seemed that one of them was supposed to rescue the Christmas cake. Each of them thought the other was supposed to save it, but it had gone up in smoke along with the house. One of them—I think it was Phillip, but I couldn't tell them apart—turned to me and said, "You know, this has been a hell of a day for me. Everything's gone wrong." He expressed himself well for a seven-year-old. I guess the cake was the last straw.

Meeting Joe DiMaggio

One year, I was playing Dean Martin in the first round of the club championship. He had me two down at the ninth hole and we stopped in the bar for a drink. Joe DiMaggio, a guest of one of the members, was standing at the bar, and we were introduced to him. Dean was very impressed. So much so that his golf game went to hell, and I ended up beating him. He asked me why I didn't get excited when I met Joe DiMaggio, and I explained to him that in 1927, I had my picture taken with Babe Ruth. To me, Joe DiMaggio was just another ball player.

Humphrey Bogart

One night about ten o'clock, I was standing at the Lakeside bar alone, talking to Eddie, the bartender.

Humphrey Bogart walked in and ordered a martini. He was wearing a topcoat and I noticed he had a knife sticking in his back, and called it to his attention. He asked me to pull the knife out, and I did. He had a slight flesh wound in his back. Eddie got his first aid kit, wiped the wound and bandaged it. I asked Bogie who stuck the knife in his back. He thought for a minute and said, "Probably someone who doesn't like me." That made sense to me so I didn't ask him any more about it.

The Night Duke Wayne Came Out To Play

Author and screenwriter James Edward Grant was a neighbor of mine and also a Lakeside member. He was my favorite bridge partner, and one afternoon we were playing bridge with Duke Wayne and John Ford, the director. Jimmy and Duke were close friends, as Jimmy had written many of his pictures. After the bridge game, Duke went home to Jimmy's house for dinner, and I went to my house.

After dinner, I walked around the corner to Jimmy's. Duke, Jimmy, and Jimmy's wife, Josephine, were sitting at the dining room table, and the window was open. I walked up to the window and asked Josephine if Jimmy could come out and play. Josephine was very direct and told me in no uncertain terms that Jimmy *could not* come out and play. Duke then asked her if *he* could go out and play. She gave him permission and was apparently glad to get rid of him.

Duke and I walked up to Alphonse's, a local Toluca Lake restaurant. We sat at the bar next to an ex-prize fighter, Tommy Coleman, who drank straight bourbon out of a shot glass. Some man we didn't know came up to the bar and started pestering Duke, who was trying his best to handle the situation, but the guy wouldn't leave him alone, and finally stuck his face into Duke's. I don't think Tommy Coleman's left hand moved more than six inches, but he knocked the guy twenty feet across the room onto the floor. Tommy then held up his right hand with the shot glass still full of bourbon and said, "Look, I never spilled a drop." He then tossed off the drink and Duke ordered him another. Duke shook his head, turned to Tommy and said, "You're just like the parts I play." We had no trouble the rest of the evening.

Howard Hughes Owes Me 80 Cents

Howard Hughes decided that he wanted to break 80. He would only play if he could start at seven o'clock in the morning, and he wouldn't play Saturday or Sunday. He talked me into playing with him so he would have somebody to sign his card when he broke eighty. The first week he didn't come too close, but he did show improvement. Each day at the ninth hole he would borrow a dime from me and call his office from the pay phone. Howard never carried any money, and thought that the club telephone switchboard was tapped. We played the next Monday and Tuesday, and on Wednesday he finally broke 80. He had 78. He made me sign his card.

He never came back to Lakeside. I don't think he ever played golf again. He had accomplished his purpose. I never saw him again, and when he died, there was a lot of controversy over his will, or "wills." As far as I could find out, there was no mention of the eighty cents he owed me in any of them, so I guess he still owes me eighty cents. I'm not mad—maybe he just forgot.

W.C. Fields

W.C. Fields had a house on Toluca Lake and occasionally walked over to the club to sit in the bar and have a few drinks. One night it was raining, and Fields came in the back door. He had a yachting cap on his head, a bottle of gin in each hand, and was soaking wet. Instead of walking over that night, he had decided to row across the lake and had fallen out of his boat. He placed the two bottles of gin on the mantelpiece and started to dry himself by the fire. He turned to the members seated around the fireplace and, pointing to the two bottles of gin, delivered a classic W.C. Fields explanation: "Storm at sea. Lost my ship but saved my cargo."

The Grace Hayes Lodge

Peter Lind Hayes was also a member of the Lakeside Golf Club. He had gone to school with my wife during their New Rochelle days. He was married to Mary Healy, and the four of us became good friends. His mother, Grace, owned the Grace Hayes Lodge on Ventura Boulevard.

It was a supper club. Peter was the emcee and did comedy monologues. Mary sang. The Lodge was a hangout for many TV and movie stars, and Grace had a way of getting them to perform in the show. It saved her hiring other actors and paying them.

One night, a funny-looking drummer came in with two other musicians. He had a new song and wanted to try it out in front of an audience. Grace let him do it at the dinner show. She didn't like the song or the performance and told him he couldn't work the late show. He and his musicians left. They were very disappointed. His name was Spike Jones and the song was, "Der Fuehrer's Face." Soon after, it became a best seller. Spike Jones ended up with a thirty-piece band and soon had his own television show. I think Grace guessed wrong that time.

* * *

One night it was Peter's birthday, and Grace decided to give him a surprise birthday party at his house. My job was to play golf with him at Lakeside and keep him there until all the guests had arrived at his house. My wife and I drove him home and all his friends jumped out of the woodwork yelling, "Surprise!" Among the guests were Bob and Delores Hope, Desi and Lucy Arnaz, Henry Fonda, Rudy Vallee, and Jackie Cooper.

It was a great party until Grace announced that the whole group would go to the Lodge to cut Peter's birthday cake. We all went to the Lodge, which, for a slow night, suddenly turned into standing room only. Grace sure knew how to fill up her Lodge. Peter had another idea.

At the end of the evening he went to all the tables and signed all the drink checks. Grace was furious, but Peter told her to take the money out of his salary. Grace pointed out that she didn't pay Peter a salary. Peter said, "Maybe if you paid me a salary you wouldn't have this problem." I forgot how it all worked out, but it was a fun night. Bob Hope, Desi and Lucy and others got up and performed. Even Henry Fonda got up and sang, "Jeepers Creepers." He was really good … almost as good as Spike Jones.

Johnny Downs

Johnny Downs, who as a child had starred in the *Our Gang* comedies, and his wife, June, were also friends of ours. Along with Peter and Mary, we would go to each other's houses and play poker. Our game was seven card stud, but we had a special rule. You sat next to your wife and whenever she got stuck, you could look at her "hole" cards and tell her what to do. One night Johnny and June wanted to play poker, but the rest of us were unavailable. Johnny and June decided to go to a poker parlor in Gardena and play with the gamblers. He sat next to June, and on the second hand she showed him her "hole" cards and asked him what to do. They were thrown out immediately. It seems that the gambling house had its own rules, too.

One day, Johnny was called before his Draft Board. He was told that he was being drafted into the Army. Johnny said they couldn't do that because he had a wife and child. The Draft Board looked at his record which showed he was single. He had not notified the Board when he got married. The Draft Board asked how they were supposed to know that he was married if he didn't notify them. Johnny pointed out that his wedding was in all the papers, but they told him the Draft Board didn't work that way. However, they did change him from 1-A to 3-A.

Johnny was still afraid. He heard that farmers would not be drafted, so he bought some land in the San Fernando Valley and started growing things. He raised crops and took them to the market to sell. He worked very hard. Then he heard that war-plant workers would not be drafted, so he got a job at Lockheed building P-38's. He worked the graveyard shift from midnight to eight a.m. He would then farm from nine a.m. to six p.m., grab some sleep, and report to Lockheed. Then he heard that actors would not be drafted, so he accepted a part in a picture. He worked from nine a.m. to six p.m. on the picture. Then he rushed to the farm, and farmed for a few hours before reporting to Lockheed. I don't know when he slept … or what he was trying to prove. Peter explained it to me. He said that Johnny found out that the Army would not draft corpses, so Johnny was trying to kill himself.

Shotgun Britton And The Colonel

One of the Lakeside members was Shotgun Britton. He was a makeup man, and was from Texas. He always wore tailor-made clothes and smoked huge, black cigars which he referred to as "heaters." They always smelled like a sewer. And, of course, being from Texas, he always talked in a loud voice.

When Shotgun was drafted, he became a private in the Air Force, and was assigned to a theater in New York City where the Air Force was putting on a show and needed a makeup man. Private or not, Shotgun had his uniforms tailor-made. His commanding officer was a colonel, and Shotgun spent most of his two years on Broadway driving his colonel crazy. Shotgun was always cramming his "heaters" in the colonel's mouth, and he kept telling the colonel that after the war he would invite him to Lakeside to play golf with all his friends like Bob Hope, Bing Crosby, Humphrey Bogart, etc.

Now, usually privates want the war to end so they can slug their colonel without getting court martialed. In Shotgun's case, it was just the reverse. The colonel could not wait for the war to end so he could slug Shotgun without getting court martialed. The war ended, and the colonel showed up at Lakeside with his brother—at least he said it was his brother. The "brother" was under treatment in a Veteran's Hospital. He had been shell-shocked. He arrived wearing sneakers and faded blue fatigues. He had an old set of wooden-shafted clubs.

The colonel and his "brother" challenged Shotgun and Dr. Dodd, his partner, to a hundred dollar Nassau. The "brother" also had a bad case of the shakes, and once in a while kicked his golf ball into a better lie. Somehow, he managed to shoot the first nine in thirty-six. And Shotgun was two down at the end of nine when they went into the bar for a drink. The "brother" started to shake severely, and the colonel decided to take him back to the hospital. He asked Shotgun for the hundred dollars that he had won on the first nine, but Shotgun said they must wait till the match was over. The colonel disagreed, and during the argument, Shotgun accused the colonel's "brother" of cheating. The "brother" heard Shotgun say this and had a sudden spasm and fell to the floor unconscious. Dr. Dodd immediately attended him and kept sending Shotgun for hot towels and water. It was all to no avail, and Dr. Dodd finally pronounced the man dead. The colonel accused Shotgun of killing his "brother" and Shotgun was terrified. Suddenly the "brother's" eyes started to flutter. Shotgun got down on his knees and begged the "brother" to speak to him. The man finally did, and whispered in a low voice, "You owe my brother a hundred dollars." The colonel had gotten even with Shotgun for the entire war. He did a wonderful job.

From Broadway To Lakeside

The first Broadway show that Mom and Dad ever took me to was *Showboat*. Charlie Wininger played Captain Andy. Other cast members were Irene Dunne, Helen Morgan, and Paul Robeson. Charlie and his wife, Blanch Ring, were friends of Dad and Mom, and they visited the house from time to time. Years later, when I joined Lakeside, Charlie Wininger had a locker about five spots up the aisle from me. My locker mate was Frank Borzage, the film director, and we played a lot of golf together. Whenever we finished a round of golf, we would sit in the locker aisle and play cards. Frank's favorite card game was "Pitch." One day in 1941, we were playing "Pitch" and Frank started to talk about W.C. Fields. He mentioned that Fields had started out in Vaudeville as a juggler. I told him that Charlie Wininger had also started out in Vaudeville as a juggler. Frank disagreed with me. He said Charlie had started out as a song and dance man, and that he had never juggled at all.

During the conversation, Charlie had walked in from the shower, and had a towel wrapped around his waist. Frank had his back to Charlie and didn't know he was there. I told Frank to turn around and look. When Frank turned, Charlie had his head in the locker, but his left arm was extended into the aisle. Without even looking at his left hand, Charlie was juggling two golf balls and a rolled up pair of socks. Frank was flabbergasted. Charlie turned out of the locker, concluded his "act" and took a bow. He then handed the golf balls and socks to Frank and said, "If you see Fields, give him these and see if he can do it."

Why Dean Martin Wouldn't Play Cards at Lakeside

One day, after finishing a round of golf, Frank Borzage and I were sitting in our locker aisle playing "Pitch" with Jimmy MacLarnen, the former boxing champion, and Pete DePaolo, the racecar driver who won the Indy 500 in 1925. Dean Martin came by and we invited him to join us. He refused to do so, saying that he never played cards with his friends. Pete demanded to know why, and reluctantly Dean picked up a deck of cards, shuffled the deck, and asked Pete to cut. Pete did so and Dean dealt 5 poker hands face down on the table. We turned over our hands one by one. Pete had 4 tens, I had 4 jacks, Frank had 4 queens, and Jimmy had 4 kings. Dean then turned his own hand over, and had 4 aces. That's why he wouldn't play cards with his friends. We agreed with him.

My Locker Buddy

George Gobel joined Lakeside in the late 40's. At that time, there was a shortage of lockers. I had a double locker, and George moved in with me. We became good friends and played a lot of golf together. We also had a lot of drinks together. George was very good at drinking. George was also very smart. Whenever he felt he had had one too many, he would put his car keys in the bar cash register and let another member drive him home.

One Saturday, we were supposed to play at ten in the morning. I went over to the club early for breakfast, and at nine-thirty I got a phone call from George. He asked me if I could come and get him, and then explained very carefully that he had four cars, but that they were all in the Lakeside parking lot, and all the keys were in the cash register. I got the keys from the bartender, picked out one of his cars, and went and got him. Apparently George had had a full week of drinking.

George Gobel, President Nixon and the Golf Ball

Every club has a member who arranges everything that goes on whether you want him to or not. Lakeside had just such a member. We called him "Busy Bill." After Nixon was elected President, Bob Hope brought him out to Lakeside for a round of golf. "Busy Bill" learned about this, and started to make arrangements. He called George Gobel to see if he wanted to fill out the Nixon/Hope foursome. George knew that this was just another arrangement that "Busy Bill" couldn't arrange, but he came over anyway because he wanted to see a President "close-up." He and "Busy Bill" ended up playing behind the Nixon/Hope foursome. Bob had made his own arrangements.

After the round, Hope and Nixon were having drinks in the locker room, surrounded by members. George had some difficulty getting into his locker to change his shoes. About that time, Robert, the locker boy, asked Hope if he would care for some hors d'oeuvres. Hope looked apprehensive as we had a rule at Lakeside that no food was to be served in the locker room. He turned to Nixon and asked, "Would you care for something to eat, Mr. President?" Nixon responded, "No, I don't want to put anyone to any trouble." Hope and the members breathed a sigh of relief, but George, who never liked the food rule anyway, turned to the President and said, "You had to spoil it for all of us." Nixon looked at George, and Hope quickly introduced them. Nixon was quick on the up-take and told George he was very happy to meet him. He then said he had never missed George's

TV show. George hadn't been on the air for two years, but he didn't mention that.

Nixon asked George to join them for a drink. George hesitated, explaining that if Nixon bought him one, he'd have to buy the next round, then Hope would buy a round, and George would end up tipsy, and that Alice would be mad at him for getting home late. Also, he didn't think that Alice would buy the excuse that he was delayed because he was having a drink with the President of the United States. Nixon said he would handle that personally. If George would get Alice on the phone, he would talk to her. "Busy Bill" rushed off to get the telephone. While he was gone, Nixon gave George a golf ball with the Presidential Seal on it. George was most appreciative. "Busy Bill" returned with the telephone and announced he had Alice Gobel on the line. Nixon took the phone and introduced himself to Alice. He asked her to excuse George for being late, explaining that he had asked George to stay as a personal favor. He then told Alice that he had had a very enjoyable round of golf at Lakeside and that he had almost had a hole-in-one. He said he had given the golf ball that he had used to George, and that George would bring it home to Alice. He handed the phone to George and got up to leave. George asked Alice to hang on a minute, and said good-bye to Nixon.

Everybody left except "Busy Bill," who told George, "See how I fixed you up." George said, "Sure you fixed me up. I was going to give this ball to a broad in New York, and now I have to take it home to Alice." "Busy

Bill" left, and George was trying to explain to Alice that she had really been talking to the President of the United States, and not Rich Little. During the conversation, Nixon suddenly reappeared by himself. He had another golf ball with the Presidential Seal on it. He handed it to George and whispered, "Here's another ball for the broad in New York." I guess President Nixon wasn't such a bad guy after all.

Jimmy Fidler And The Mystery Stars

Jimmy Fidler, the Hollywood columnist, was also a Lakeside member. He won a few bucks from me playing golf, and then offered me a job. He was starting a program for underprivileged children called "The National Kids' Day Foundation." In order to raise money for the Foundation, he had decided to put a mystery star contest on his weekly radio program. His radio audience was asked to identify the mystery star each week, send a contribution to the Foundation, and also send in a slogan that would help promote National Kids' Day. Jimmy arranged for the stars, and I wrote the clues. I would go to the stars' homes with a recorder to tape their clues for the show. Secrecy was of the utmost importance, and the stars were most cooperative. But some interesting things did happen.

When I went to Joan Crawford's house, she mispronounced one word. I called it to her attention and suggested she record it again. She thought she had pronounced it correctly, and finally called her lawyer, Greg

Bautzer, about the pronunciation. He agreed with me, and Joan immediately re-recorded her spot.

Jeanette MacDonald also changed one word in my clue which, by the way, I still remember. I had written:

My husband's a man with two first names
No, it isn't Harry James
With this one clue you should go far
It's also true of my favorite co-star.

Jeanette changed "favorite" to "frequent." I didn't correct her. I'm sure she was right as she knew Nelson Eddy much better than I did.

One night, I went to Roy Rogers' house. He and Dale were having dinner, so I set my recorder up in their den. Three of their children came in and I let them talk into the recorder so they could hear their voices play back. One little girl was very impressed and decided to tell me a family secret. Before I could cut her off, she told me that her mother was going to have a new baby, but no one was allowed to know because they had promised to tell Louella Parsons first[1]. Roy walked in the door just as she finished the story. He turned and left without a word. In two minutes his press agent came into the den, visibly shaken. I told

---

1 During the evolution of the entertainment industry, the most important publicity that could be had was from a newspaper columnist's article. Jimmy Fidler and Louella Parsons were two of the most influential and popular gossip and entertainment columnists of the early 20th century. Fidler and Parsons were in constant competition to be the most popular gossip columnist of the time.

him the secret was safe with me, that I was not one of Fidler's reporters, and that I would not tell him. It was a Thursday night and they were trying to save the "scoop" for Louella's Sunday night radio show. I told him I was sure that their "secret" would not last until Sunday, and suggested they call Louella immediately and tell her what happened. Then they could lock me in their closet until Sunday night because I knew I would get blamed if Fidler found out. They called Louella, and she put it in her newspaper column the next day. She knew it would leak out, too. Roy taped his spot and I didn't get locked in the closet.

PART 3

Career

CHAPTER 8

Film and Early Career

An Introduction by Adrienne

DAD HAD BEEN hired by the Motion Picture Production Code Board by way of a telegram he'd received on May 11, 1939, at Georgetown University:

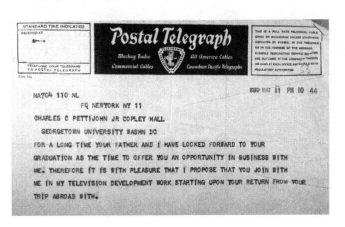

STANDARD TIME INDICATED
RECEIVED AT

Postal Telegraph

Mackay Radio   All America Cables
Commercial Cables   Canadian Pacific Telegraphs

TELEPHONE YOUR TELEGRAMS
TO POSTAL TELEGRAPH

NA704 110 NL   1939 MAY 11 PM 10 44

FQ NEWYORK NY 11

CHARLES C PETTIJOHN JR COPLEY HALL

GEORGETOWN UNIVERSITY WASHN DC

FOR A LONG TIME YOUR FATHER AND I HAVE LOOKED FORWARD TO YOUR

GRADUATION AS THE TIME TO OFFER YOU AN OPPORTUNITY IN BUSINESS WITH

ME. THEREFORE IT IS WITH PLEASURE THAT I PROPOSE THAT YOU JOIN WITH

ME IN MY TELEVISION DEVELOPMENT WORK STARTING UPON YOUR RETURN FROM YOUR

TRIP ABROAD WITH.

Courtland Smith Telegram (front)

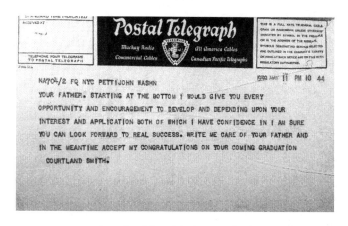

Courtland Smith Telegram (back)

Joe Breen And The Motion Picture Production Code

In September 1940, I reported to work for Joe Breen on the motion picture production staff. I was one of seven editors. Two editors read each script, and the number one editor contacted the producer of the picture to advise him if it contained any violations of the production code. If you did your job properly and got along with the producer, you wouldn't have to make any cuts in the finished film. During the first year, I was the second reader on all my assignments. I was confined to cheap westerns, cartoons, and short subjects like the old "Three Stooges" comedies.

Finally, Mr. Breen decided I could become a first reader, and he let me do *The Road to Singapore* because I played golf with Bob Hope and Bing Crosby. I guess I did okay, because he let me do all the "Road" pictures. A big thrill was when he let me do *Citizen Kane,* and I got to work with Orson Welles, who was known as "The Boy Wonder." I think he was only a couple of years older than I was, so I told him I was a "boy wonder" too. We got along. When the picture was finished, Welles brought it to our projection room for screening. The whole staff, including Mr. Breen, viewed the picture. It was acceptable from our standpoint, and was also a brilliant film, years ahead of its time. We all congratulated him, and then he asked us all a question. "What did 'rosebud' mean?" I waited for someone else to speak, but no one did. Then Orson asked me directly. I told him that I thought "rosebud" meant the only time in Citizen Kane's life that he was happy. Orson was proud of me...I had given him the right answer. I was proud of me, too.

Apparently Mr. Breen was satisfied because he let me do Charlie Chaplin's next picture, *Monsieur Verdoux.* Once again the entire staff viewed the film. There were no edits, and Chaplin told Breen that he had enjoyed working with me. Chaplin turned in his seat to shake my hand, and inadvertently hooked the wire to our projection room wall clock. The clock pulled off the wall and hit Chaplin in the head. He wasn't hurt, but it scared the hell out of him. It scared the hell out of me, too.

Breen then let me try Sam Goldwyn. The picture was, *The Pride of the Yankees.* It was the story of Lou Gehrig. I had to go to Goldwyn's private projection room to see it. Laura Greenhouse went with me. She always attended screenings as it was her job to fill out the involved production code report. These reports were important whenever the industry was attacked by various groups. For example, every occupation or trade in a picture was noted, and the portrayal was classified favorable or unfavorable. These statistics protected the motion picture producers against unfounded attacks.

If law enforcement agencies, doctors, carpenters, clergymen, or any other trades or professions claimed that they were portrayed unfairly, Laura's reports gave us the real figures. She carried a little light on her clipboard to make her notes during the screenings. Mr. Goldwyn came into the projection room and told Laura to turn off her light. I started to explain to Mr. Goldwyn why she needed the light. I used "policemen" as an example, but Goldwyn interrupted me. He said, "There are no policemen in this picture ... turn off the light." Laura turned off the light. We looked at the picture, and it was a very, very good film. No edits were necessary. When we got back to the office, Laura filled out her report from memory.

I mentioned Dr. Lee De Forest earlier, but while working for Mr. Breen, I got a chance to meet him at a Motion Picture Association dinner. I told him how we used to sit around and "watch" the radio, and thanked him for inventing the television tube. He told me that the "tube" was only one of many inventions and that he liked most of his other ones better. We were standing next to a television set at the time. He put his hand on the set. Then the great inventor looked at me and said,

"This is De Forest's prime evil." He knew his literature, and had a great sense of humor. Lately, I've been wondering if he wasn't wrong about his invention. What do you think?

Clark Gable

The Motion Picture Producer's Association and Central Casting had office space in a building on the corner of Hollywood Boulevard and Western Avenue. The building was owned by Louis B. Mayer. One day, Mr. Mayer was attending a meeting in the building when there was a minor earthquake. Mayer beat everybody else out of the building. I guess he knew something.

At street level there was a combination drug store and lunch counter, and I ate there frequently. One day they hired a new girl to work the lunch counter. She told us her name was Miriam and that she had come to Hollywood from Dubuque, Iowa. Unlike many girls, she told us she did not come to Hollywood to be a movie star, although her life's ambition was to meet Clark Gable.

Two or three weeks later, Gable came into the building to attend a meeting. During a break he stuck his nose in my office to say hello. I told him about Miriam and he agreed to walk down to the drug store with me since he wanted a milk shake anyway. We sat at the counter. Miriam was very busy, saw me out of the corner of her eye, but didn't notice Gable. I told her we wanted a couple of chocolate shakes. She mixed them and put them in the blender while waiting on other customers at the same time. Then she put two glasses in front of us, turned and got my shake and poured it into the glass. She reached back and turned to pour in Gable's glass. As the container was in the air she looked up and saw Gable's face for the first time. The container kept going. She missed the glass and poured the shake all over Gable. Then she screamed and ran out the back door. The manager brought Gable a towel, and he wiped himself off. Then the manager went out back to look for Miriam. He couldn't find her. He came back, apologized to Gable, and made him another shake. He didn't charge us for any of them. Gable was very gracious and gave the manager a five dollar tip for Miriam. Miriam never came back. She never got the five-dollar bill. She had a week's pay coming but she never picked that up, either.

CHAPTER 9

The Navy

An Introduction by Adrienne

THE OUTBREAK OF World War II interrupted the lives of many people throughout the world. My Dad's was no exception. However, as you will learn in the following stories, his induction into the military was a bit unusual because of his affiliation with the entertainment industry. And his participation within the military was a bit unusual probably because he was a Pettijohn.

Dennis Morgan Made Me Join the Navy But Forgot to Come with Me

One day in December, 1943, Dennis Morgan, Jack Carson, and some others from the Warner Brothers clique came over to Lakeside for lunch. Dennis had a clipping from the Los Angeles Times. It was an ad placed by the United States Navy saying they had openings for a thousand ensigns. I think the only condition was two years of college. Dennis decided we should join the navy, and he talked me into it. We agreed to go down to the recruiting office after lunch and fill out the application. Then the phone rang at the end of the bar and one of the other Warner Brothers actors, Ronald Reagan, answered it. It was for Dennis, and Reagan handed him the phone. Dennis was needed back at the Warner Brothers studio for a pick-up shot. He told me to go to the recruiting office and that he would meet me there later.

Dennis went back to Warners, and Reagan didn't exactly disappear into obscurity. Thirty-seven years later he reappeared as President of the United States.

Dennis never showed up at the recruiting office, but I filled out the form and became an ensign all by myself. Then the navy took over. Because I lived in Hollywood, they sent me to New York for forty-two days of indoctrination school at Fort Schuyler. I learned to salute. They then decided I needed more training, and sent me to Treasure Island in San Francisco Bay. They put me on a PC which was a one hundred and seventy-five foot sub-chaser.

I was an extra officer, and I quickly learned to say "deck" instead of "floor," and "bulkhead" instead of "wall." Windows became "portholes." Obviously, I needed more training, so they sent me to submarine-chaser training school in Miami, Florida.

On the way from San Francisco to Miami, I stopped at Lakeside. Dennis Morgan was at the bar. He was wearing the uniform of a Lieutenant Commander in the navy. He had lots of medals and ribbons on his chest. He was making a picture at Warner Brothers and was playing the hero. The Warner Brothers wardrobe department had created a striking, tailor-made uniform for him. I was wearing my fatigues. Dennis looked much better than I did. Warner Brothers promoted people faster than the navy did.

I finally reached Miami. I had now driven across the North American continent three times without coming to grips with an ocean, which is where I thought the navy worked.

When I finished at Miami, I finally got orders to report to a ship. It was a Corvette—the PG-68. It was berthed in Staten Island, New York, so I drove up there. The Corvette was a reverse lend-lease Canadian ship. I reported to the Captain who examined my Navy record and didn't seem too impressed. He made me his Supply Officer, and I had to order food. I'd never done that before... our housekeeper had always done it. But I learned.

We made two convoy escort runs between Cuba and Staten Island. At last I got to sail on an ocean. Then we were switched to the North Atlantic run. For this my Captain claimed his Corvette rated a Jeep. As the ship's Supply Officer, I went to the Transportation Office at the Staten Island base to pick it up, but the Transportation Officer refused to give it to me. He claimed the Corvette did not rate a Jeep. My Captain got mad at me. He wanted transportation when we got to England. I solved the problem. One night I gave the crane operator on the dock a bottle of scotch, and he picked up *my* car and put it aboard the ship behind the stack where the *Jeep* should be. I covered it with canvas. Just before we got to England, our convoy was attacked. A German plane fired at us. I guess the German pilot was dumb—he was supposed to blow up ships *in* the convoy—not the escort ships. Anyway, his bullets shot out the windshield of my car. I believe that I am the only officer in naval history whose 1940 Ford two-door sedan was wounded in the middle of the Atlantic Ocean.

When we got to England, the Captain got the windshield fixed and used it to drive around the countryside. He wouldn't let me drive my own car, but we did get along better after the incident.

Captain Queeg I Ain't

After we won the war, the PG-68 was returned to Canada, and I came up for reassignment. For some strange reason my Captain had recommended me for command. I thought he had made a mistake and called it to his attention. He said he had not made a mistake, and that he had recommended me on purpose. He felt that no other Captain should have to suffer by having me as a Junior Officer. I took command of the PC-582. It was in dry dock in the Brooklyn Navy Yard. I think it was in December of 1945. The ship's complement was five officers and twelve men. I was ordered to take the ship to Norfolk, West Virginia, and report to Admiral Gatch. I didn't have enough men to put to sea, and the Bureau of Naval Personnel was too busy to send me any. Across the street from the Brooklyn Navy yard was the Navy Receiving Station. It was packed with sailors awaiting reassignment. Most of them had been there so long they wanted to get out. I made friends with a few of the sailors, showed them my ship, and asked if they'd like to be on my crew. Strangely enough, a lot of them wanted to.

I got a yeoman to steal some forms from the Receiving Station, and we typed out orders, in triplicate of course, assigning my "volunteers" to duty on the PC-582. I then forged the Duty Officer's signature on the orders and handed them to the Master at Arms at the Receiving Station. He assembled my "volunteers"—not noticing that they had already been assembled—and marched them across the street to the PC-582. We put out immediately to Norfolk.

Upon our arrival the next day, there was an urgent message from Admiral Gatch to report to him in person, immediately. The Admiral was very gruff. It seemed that I had the only ship in the entire Eastern Sea Frontier with a full complement of men. I played dumb—which was very easy for me—explaining that I had requested my men from the Bureau of Personnel, and that they had been sent to my ship from the Brooklyn Receiving Station. I don't think he bought my explanation, but he had his own problem and I could be useful to him. It seems that he had a portable dry dock in Bermuda that he wanted towed to Norfolk. Procedure was to have the Coast Guard tow the dry dock. The Coast Guard didn't want to do it. It seems it was the hurricane season and towing a dry dock around Cape Hatteras was too risky at that time of year. The Admiral did not want to wait. He sent a navy tug to Bermuda to tow the dock to Norfolk. When they got off of Cape Hatteras a storm came up and the dry dock broke loose and capsized … just like the Coast Guard had told him it would. It became a "menace to navigation" floating around in the sea lanes. When something becomes a "menace to navigation" it is supposed to be reported to the Coast Guard and they handle the problem. As you can see, the Admiral could not report this to the Coast Guard. Instead, he used me and the PC-582, the only ship in the navy with a full complement of men. He told me to go find the dry dock and blow it up. Of course I said, "Aye, aye, sir" and immediately put to sea.

Strangely enough, we actually found the dry dock upside down about a hundred miles off shore. The sea was very, very rough. We shot at it with our three inch gun, but it was either too rough to hit it or the shells made no impression. I tried dropping depth charges set to go off at fifty feet beside the dock. The depth charges made no impression either, and we ran out of depth charges. Finally, the dry dock broke in half of its own accord. Half of it sank, but the other half was still a "menace." I decided the best thing to do was put a big red flag and a light on the floating half. At least other ships could see it. Three men volunteered to paddle over in a life raft and do the job.

One of them was a Machinist Mate Third Class named Woodall. He got aboard the dock with great difficulty and secured the flag and the light. It became too rough for the raft to get near the dry dock to pick up Woodall. He finally dove in to swim back to the ship even though I told all three to stay out of the water. I was on the flying bridge screaming at him when a shark surfaced and started to glide after him. We had a Jacob's ladder at the stern of the ship for him to climb up. I fell off the flying bridge just as the shark passed under it, chasing Woodall. I had a knife in my belt, and I landed on top of the shark...I was terrified. I stuck the knife in the shark, then I climbed over Woodall's back and beat him up the ladder. Some of the crew and the other officers saw what happened. They thought I was very brave ... they thought I had jumped off the bridge onto the shark. I explained that I didn't jump, that I had slipped. They wouldn't believe me. They liked the "jump" story better.

We decided to go back to Norfolk. Just as we were leaving, the other half of the dry dock sank of its own accord. The "menace to navigation" no longer existed. Our mission had been accomplished.

Back in Norfolk, the story about the shark got out, and I got a Letter of Commendation from the Navy Department. A copy was placed in my file at the Bureau of Personnel in Washington. About a month after the dry dock incident, I ran into a buoy in Chesapeake Bay. I guess I wasn't paying attention and the buoy chain bent one of my propellers. I had to go back into dry dock to get the propeller straightened. I got a letter of Admonition from the navy for my negligence. A copy was also placed in my file at the Bureau of Personnel in Washington. Through some curious coincidence, both my Letter of Admonition and my Letter of Commendation were dated the same day. I think I'm the only United States Naval Officer to whom that ever happened.

Finally Admiral Gatch got tired of me and transferred me to Newport, Rhode Island, as a school ship for the Naval War College. I was delighted. I had always wanted to have my own yacht in Newport during the "season."

Meanwhile, my daughter Muffy was a month old, and I had never seen her. I called my wife in New Rochelle, told her I was on my way to Newport, and would stop at the Westchester Country Club Beach Club to see her. To go from Norfolk to Newport, you are supposed to set a course around Long Island Sound, and also inform the navy of your departure and estimated arrival times. The navy liked to know where their ships were at all times, and when they were supposed to get where they were going. But I wanted to see my new daughter. I decided to go into New York Harbor, go up the East River, under the Whitestone Bridge, and down Long Island Sound to Rye Beach.

There was a dense fog in New York when I hit the entrance to Ambrose Channel. I couldn't see the buoys. Other ships were waiting for the fog to clear so they could enter the harbor. I couldn't wait. I looked at the radar scope and it showed two beautiful lines of "pips." They looked like the port and starboard buoys of Ambrose Channel. I steered course between them and ran the ship aground in the mud. The radar scope had played a trick on me. It had picked up the port buoys of Ambrose Channel and starboard buoys of Sandy Hook Channel. In between those buoys was mud, and that's where I was. The tide was going out. The fog lifted and everyone could see what I had done.

All hands came out on deck. I told them all to go to one side of the ship and then walk back and forth from side to side to make the ship rock. The motion worked the ship loose from the mud, and I was able to back off. My senior enlisted man was Chief Motor Machinist, Ken Place. He was regular navy and a career man. We got along fairly well, although he was somewhat annoyed with my lack of knowledge of the sea. He came up on the bridge and asked me how I knew enough to have the crew move back and forth to rock the ship. I told him the truth … I had read it in *Collier's Magazine*. It was a story about Tug Boat Annie, written by Norman Reilly Raine. The same thing had happened to her, and that's how she had gotten her ship loose. So it worked for me, too. Chief Place didn't like my answer. He was hoping that it was something I'd learned in *his* navy.

We finally got to the Beach Club, and I got to spend two hours with my new daughter. Then we finished our trip to Newport. I gave all the members of my crew as much leave and liberty that I could possibly get away with. They were all very happy, and the business of my running the ship aground in New York Harbor was never mentioned.

Model of the PC-582 I commanded [1]

---

1   The military will issue a model of his ship to its captain, but not all ship captains are bestowed this honor.

CHAPTER 10

Television

Universal International

AFTER I GOT out of the navy, I went back to work for Joe Breen. After a couple of months, I got the "studio bug" and wanted to work in production. I talked to Mr. Breen, and he arranged a job for me working at Universal as "contact man" with the Motion Picture Production Code. Bill Goetz and Leo Spitz, who owned International Pictures, had just merged with Universal. They hired Bill Dozier to manage the lot for them. Dozier's first wife had once been Dad's secretary, and I had met him several times. Goetz and Spitz also knew Dad, but I had never met them. Anyway, Dozier and Breen arranged for me to meet with Bill Goetz. He was very courteous, asked about Dad, and then offered me the job. He said he would not pay me a lot of money, and asked how much Joe Breen was paying me. I was making six hundred dollars a month and told Mr. Goetz, "Six hundred." He said he would pay me the same ... no more. That was great with me. It opened the door to production.

I went to work on a Monday. The next Monday was pay day and my check added up to six hundred dollars. I wondered why they paid in advance until the next Monday, when I got another six hundred dollar check. The third Monday I got another one. I started to panic. Sis and I talked it over, and decided to live off one check and put the other three in the bank against the day that Goetz would ask for his money back. I finally took my "problem" to Joe Breen and asked his advice. He told me to shut up and keep the money.

After seven months, there was a meeting at the Producers' Association. The bottom had fallen out of the motion picture business, and drastic cuts had to be made. Joe Breen was asked to cut his fees. Breen said his fees just barely covered the Production Code Administration expenses, and that he was cutting corners at that. Goetz spoke up and said he was paying his staff too much money, pointing out that Breen had even been paying that "chump" Pettijohn six hundred dollars a week. Breen explained that he had been paying Pettijohn six hundred dollars a month, and that Goetz was the one who decided to pay him six hundred dollars a week. Then he added that Pettijohn was not a "chump" … he was getting the money … Goetz was the "chump" for paying it to him. Goetz came back to Universal and told Dozier to fire me. Of course Dozier had to. I was very disappointed, but what the hell … I was seven months ahead of schedule in salary.

CBS

In 1955, I was out of work again. I went to see David Selznick. He didn't have anything I could do ... as you know, my talent was limited ... but suggested I get into television. Apparently he called his friend, William S. Paley, head of CBS. Then he called me, and told me to go to CBS and see Bill Dozier, who was then Vice President Programs, CBS-Hollywood. Dozier was very courteous and called the head of Program Practices, who was out of town for three weeks. Then he said, "Well, you've read a lot of scripts, you can work in our Story Department." Bud Kaye was the CBS Television Network Story Editor and Dozier talked him into giving me a job as a reader. I thanked Dozier very much, and he asked me if I wanted to know what my salary would be. I said anything would be fine—I needed the money. He said, "Charlie, it's no six hundred dollars a week." He was right ... it was eighty-five dollars a week. I was glad to get it. I always liked Bill Dozier. He hired me twice and only fired me once.

The CBS Story Department

As a reader, I worked with two other readers, Helen and Sonia. We were all in the same room, and were reading material submitted for *Climax* and *Playhouse 90*. We read books, magazine stories, scripts, treatments, and most anything a reputable literary agent brought in. Each piece of material was synopsized in about two pages, and the reader would add his or her own comments and recommendations. Each reader felt rewarded

inwardly when a producer bought one of his or her recommendations. The "reward" was not reflected in our
salary check.

About this time I became involved in the creation of
our neighborhood Little League, and ended up coaching
one of the baseball teams. Bud Kaye, my boss, told me
to try to find a Little League story for *Front Row Center*
(a variety show that aired on the DuMont Television
Network). I talked to many writers and agents, but none
of them could come up with a story. Bud Kaye kept bugging me. One weekend I went into the office and wrote
one myself. It was a seventeen page treatment which I
titled, "The Little League Genius." The next day I told
Bud I had found a Little League Story. He asked who
wrote it, and I told him I did. He seemed very disappointed, but said he would read it anyway. It took him
three weeks to get around to it. Then he came into my
office and told me he liked it and that he thought it was
very good. With great modesty I agreed with him. He
sent it upstairs to the producer of *Front Row Center*, and
the producer bought it.

Bud asked me if I wanted to write the teleplay, but
I was afraid to try it. I was sure the story was good,
but I didn't want to ruin it by writing a lousy teleplay. I
thought I would be better off if a good professional writer wrote the teleplay, so it would turn out to be a good
show. A good professional writer wrote the teleplay. He
threw out my title, changed my storyline, and changed
the Little League to the Pony League. The show stank.
Maybe I should have tried to write the teleplay.

* * *

Agents always stopped by the readers' office to try to get us to read their clients' material first. One agent was named Maurice "Mauri" Grashin. He heard us talking about what happened to my Little League story and asked if he could read my treatment. He liked it and told me next time to write the teleplay myself. I had written a short story for *Collier's Magazine* called "Delightful Suspicion." I liked it very much, but *Collier's* didn't. They sent it back. Sonia, one of the other readers, read it and liked it. She agreed to help me put it in teleplay form, and we wrote the teleplay together. Then we showed it to Mauri and he liked it. He took it to Universal, and they bought it for *General Electric Theater*[1] two days later. It seems they had just made a deal for Jack Benny to do an episode, and bought three or four scripts for him to pick from. He picked another one. "Delightful Suspicion" was never shot. I saw the episode that Benny had chosen. I thought it was lousy. I thought "Delightful Suspicion" would have been much better … possibly even sensational.

* * *

CBS needed the Story Department offices for the writers of the *Red Skelton Show*, so we readers became scattered around the building. I ended up with an office in

---

1   *General Electric Theater* was an anthology series, running from 1953 to 1962. Ronald Reagan was the host.

the Casting Department, and became friendly with the casting directors. Russ Trost was head of casting and lived in Burbank about a mile from me. Casting directors were always on the telephone, and for this reason Russ always took the bus back and forth to work. It was the only time he could read the scripts that he had to cast without the telephone ringing. Sometimes I would give him a ride home, but only if he had no scripts to read. At one point, the casting director who did the *Red Skelton Show* was out sick for a few weeks, and I ended up casting bit parts and extras for the *Red Skelton Show*. Of course, Russ checked my work, but at least he didn't have to do it all himself. And I enjoyed it. I got to meet a lot of agents, bit players, and extras who were always dropping into the casting office. One extra was very interesting. He kept complaining that he could never get a job because he looked too much like Marlon Brando. But he did do fairly well as a stuntman. A few years later, after I transferred to Program Practices, our paths crossed again.

One of my assignments was *Gunsmoke,* and I got on good terms with Norman MacDonnell, the producer. He was adding a new character to *Gunsmoke*, and was looking for an actor to play a half-breed Indian blacksmith. One day while I was in his office, he was looking through pictures and they included my old friend, the stuntman-extra who claimed he looked like Marlon Brando. I recommended him to Norman and he agreed to take a look. A couple of weeks later, he called me and told me that my recommendation had been cast in the part. He became a regular until the *Gunsmoke* series ended. He only disappeared into obscurity for a couple of months. Then he re-emerged as a semi-well-known movie actor. If you're curious to know who he is, his name is Burt Reynolds.

Frank Sinatra

In 1966, Frank Sinatra made a deal to do a special for Budweiser to air on CBS. Frank preferred to tape it at NBC, where he felt more at home. I was assigned to the show and went to cover the taping. I got two tickets to the air show for Sis and a neighbor who wanted to see Sinatra. After taping dress rehearsal, Sinatra came out to tape a one-minute commercial for Budweiser, who had agreed to give him a Lamborghini as a fee for the commercial. He did the commercial in one take and looked at the playback. He told the director his last speech would have been better if he'd taken it on the close up camera. The director said, "That's okay. We'll get it on the next take." Sinatra asked the director if he was going to get another car for doing another take. The director said, "No," and Frank went right to his dressing room and locked the door.

About ten minutes later, Shotgun Britton, Frank's makeup man, stuck his head out the door and motioned to me. He told me that Frank was leaving and would not tape the air show, and that I should tell whoever had to know that the tape of the dress rehearsal was all they were going to get. I went to tell the producers, but they refused to believe me. I borrowed their phone and called Sis at home and told her not to come to the air show as Sinatra would not be in it. Then the producers believed me. They went to see Frank, but unsuccessfully. He had left. They taped an air show with the guest stars and it didn't turn out too bad. Frank had been very good on the dress tape and his performance was edited into the air taping.

Playhouse 90

Dave Powers was a stage manager on *Playhouse 90*[2], and, as such, it was his responsibility to throw cues to the actors. James Gregory was a New York actor who had come to Hollywood to do his first television show. He took Dave aside early in rehearsals and asked him to bring his props to his dressing room during show breaks. He said that he had always had trouble with props and needed to practice. Dave did as he was requested. Later, Jim told Dave that he had trouble seeing his cues because of the lights, and asked Dave to give him a more swinging motion with his arm rather than just flipping his hand. Again, Dave did as requested. Finally, Jim said that he still had trouble seeing Dave and asked him if he could wear a more brightly colored shirt. Dave had a

---

2 *Playhouse 90* was an award-winning television show that ran from 1956 to 1960. The show was an innovative take on the traditional hour-long television segments that were popular at the time. *Playhouse 90* ran for ninety minutes, and portrayed a myriad of dramatic episodes that were critically acclaimed, and the show is listed on *TV Guide*'s 50 Greatest Television Shows of All Time.

sweater with red and white triangles, and he wore that. Jim seemed satisfied.

The day before air, they were on stage camera blocking. John Frankenheimer, the director, came out of the booth to re-block a scene on stage. When it was set, he told Dave to cue Jim. Dave jumped in the air and gave a long, swinging motion with his arms. Frankenheimer yelled, "Cut," and asked Dave what the hell he was doing. Didn't he know he would drive the actors crazy giving cues like that. Jim then turned to Frankenheimer and said, "John, I'm glad to hear you say that because Dave has been driving me nuts. He follows me around with a basket full of my props like I'm some kind of an idiot who doesn't know how to work with them. Every time he cues me he jumps up and down like a yoyo, and today he came out here wearing that clown suit." Dave was speechless until the whole crew burst out laughing. Jim had set Dave up beautifully. It was a hell of a good joke. Dave recovered quickly and became one of the top television directors. His credits included *The Carol Burnett Show* and *Three's Company*. Jim Gregory went on to do television regularly—you may have seen him on *Barney Miller*.

* * *

John Frankenheimer was the director of *The Snows of Kilimanjaro*. It was adapted from Ernest Hemingway's novel. One important scene took place in a safari jungle camp, and John decided that live vultures would make the scene more realistic. A trainer brought in four vultures, but they refused to perch on the limb that John wanted them on for his camera shot. The trainer solved the problem by lashing the vultures' feet to the limb. Then John decided that the vultures should flap their wings a little. He started to tape the shot and cued the trainer to wave a newspaper at the vultures. Instead of flapping, the vultures merely fell off the limb and hung upside down, completely destroying John's realism. The trainer was paid his rent for the vultures and took them home. They never appeared in *The Snows of Kilimanjaro*, but it was a pretty good show anyway.

Ed Sullivan

When I was a kid, Ed Sullivan was a sports reporter on a local newspaper, the *Port Chester Daily Item*. Port Chester was a town next to Rye, New York. He came to the house once to do a story on the major league baseball career of my Uncle Jimmy. Jimmy was then working for a bolt and nut factory in Port Chester, and played for the company team. His major league career had ended when his arm went bad. I also played a couple of rounds of golf with Ed before moving to California. Ed had left the *Port Chester Item* and eventually wrote a theatrical column for the *New York Daily News* … and from there he went on to his own television show. He would come west once in a while to tape some episodes, and I was assigned to these episodes. We did two or three shows in Las Vegas. I hadn't seen Ed for years, and we had some fun talking about Rye and Port Chester. He did one show in San Francisco that I'd like to tell you about.

We were on location on the beach under the Golden Gate Bridge, and Peggy Lee was standing in the sand at the water's edge singing a beautiful ballad. As her song finished, an aircraft carrier left Treasure Island and headed up the Golden Gate Channel on its way to sea. There were planes lined up in formation on the flight deck, and nearly a thousand sailors were standing at parade rest. It was a beautiful sight, and Byron Paul, the director, came up with a wonderful idea. He ordered the prop man to roll the credits as he wanted to super them over the shot of the carrier leaving port. When he rolled the credits, they broke, and he screamed at the prop man to hurry and fix the credit spindles. Then he yelled at the stage manager in a voice everyone could hear, "Re-cue the carrier!" Everybody broke up, but the credit spindles were repaired and Bryon got the shot before the carrier passed by under the bridge. Byron still has a video cassette of the credits rolling over the carrier.

Censors

Censors are not censors … they are anti-censors. That is, unless they work for the government. Then they are censors. If they work for motion picture or television producers, then they are nurses. Nurses are hired to raise children who would get in trouble if they didn't have a nurse. Movie and television producers are children. The Motion Picture Producers' Association hired Will Hays to help raise their "children." When I went to work for Joe Breen I became an assistant "nurse." My "children" always referred to me as their censor, and they blamed me for everything. I was responsible for about ten percent of the things I was accused of. The other ninety percent were pure fallacies. Here are some of the fallacies.

* * *

Word went around Hollywood that a man and a woman could never be shown together in a double bed. This was completely untrue. It seems that in England, the British Board of Film Censors (they worked for the government and they were real censors) would cut any scenes of a man and a woman in the same bed. We simply advised our producers that their film would be cut in England, and they might want to shoot their bedroom scene two ways if they were planning an English release. By the time the "advice" was spread around town, it became Joe Breen's fault. Many producers and writers believed that the Breen Office would cut such scenes, and therefore never even wrote or filmed them.

The State of Ohio had a censor board that always cut out scenes of someone hitting someone else over the head with any hard object such as a gun butt. We advised producers to complete such "slugs over the head" out of frame, or the State of Ohio would cut their finished picture. Cincinnati was a major film distribution exchange, and the Ohio State censors viewed and cut the films in Cincinnati. The Cincinnati exchange also shipped prints to the neighboring states such as Illinois, Indiana, Michigan, Pennsylvania, and other states that did not have political censor boards. I am sure that the film editors at the Cincinnati exchange never bothered to put the censored Ohio footage back in the prints when they shipped them to the other states. Naturally we "nurses" got blamed instead of the Ohio Censor Board.

As a television "nurse" I was also called a "censor" by the producers. Sometimes the producers used me when a star wanted to do something that the producers didn't want the star to do. George Carlin was doing a summer show at CBS, and we became friends and used to have a few drinks at Kelbo's, the bar across the street from the CBS Studio. One day he came into my office mad as hell. He wanted to know why I had nixed a young comedy team that he had recommended for his show. I knew nothing about it but I could guess what happened.

George's producer had auditioned the team and didn't like them, so the producer blamed it on the censor rather than tell George. Later, George brought the team into Kelbo's, and they did their routine. Their material was not off-color, and was acceptable from my standpoint. It also wasn't funny, so I guess the producer was right, too. It's a shame he didn't tell me first. I could've helped.

Cecil Barker produced the *Red Skelton Show*. He was my favorite producer, and became a close friend. When Red wanted to use any material that Cecil didn't like, many times he would blame it on me. But he always told me first before he told Red. Then I could make up a story to cover myself, and it kept a good relationship between the producer and the star, which resulted in better shows. I always liked better shows. It was a pleasure to contribute my little bit.

The Blacklist [3] and CBS

When my boss was transferred to New York, he promoted me to his job, and I became Director of Program Practices—Hollywood in January of 1966. I discovered that one of my subsidiary duties was a rather unpleasant one. Any performer appearing on a CBS Network show had to be cleared. Casting directors were instructed to call my office before making commitments. If a name was on the blacklist, my secretary Lorraine said, "No" and that was it.

About a year after I became Director, there was a small fire in our office right near the blacklist files. We put the fire out quickly. A day later I was talking to my Vice President in New York, and mentioned what almost happened to the blacklist. He reprimanded me for putting out the fire so soon and asked me if I had any matches. He said he would send me a lighter if I didn't. That was all I needed to know. Lorraine called maintenance for a dolly. A warehouseman brought it up to the office and helped Lorraine and me load the files. The three of us then dragged it next door to the Farmer's

---

3 During the 1940s and 1950s, Senator Joseph McCarthy upset the world of entertainment with his infamous "blacklist," which tied many performers and entertainers to communist ideas or communist sympathizers. Members of the entertainment business who were on McCarthy's blacklist were fired from their current jobs and were inhibited from getting further work until the issue was resolved. Many entertainers and performers were imprisoned during this time for their communist sympathies. McCarthy's list was eventually found to be inaccurate, but this movement still shook up Hollywood for many years.

Market where a large refuse furnace was always burning. We threw all the files in the furnace. Senator McCarthy may have hated me for this, but I felt a lot better.

The Smothers Brothers

In 1965, the Smothers Brothers arrived on the scene. They had made a few episodes of an unsuccessful film situation comedy in which Tommy played an angel, then they switched to a variety format, and Tommy never bore any resemblance to an angel again—especially as far as I was concerned. He sure hated censors. The show started off about fifty-second in the Nielsen Ratings, and after twenty shows had aired, it became the third highest rated show on television. I was delighted at the success of the show, but it was a rough trip for me. When it ended, I was replaced as Director of Program Practices. The twenty shows had caused the network to receive a total of 179 complaint letters. The next season the show received 4,361 complaint letters, and my replacement was replaced. The third year the complaint letters totaled over 34,000, and Tommy and Dickie were replaced.

Let me tell you about the twenty shows I was responsible for. Sam Taylor, my assistant, was the editor on the show, but I read every script and attended every Wednesday afternoon run-thru with Sam. The show taped on Friday night, and I usually attended all the Friday tapings. This was especially true of the last twelve shows when the musicians' strike delayed production. We ended up taping Friday night for an episode that aired on Sunday night. Each show had to be edited immediately following taping, and then the air tape had to be flown to New York, carried by a special messenger in order to air on time. Consequently, the acceptability of the material from the stand point of Program Practices was solely my decision. There was no time for my boss in New York to view it. He did not care to work on Sundays, but he sure raised hell with me every Monday morning.

One particular sketch caused me the most trouble with my boss. It was a sketch in which Tom and Dick took censors apart. I was delighted with the sketch as Tom and Dick were always taking some profession apart. If they had taken apart doctors or lawyers instead of censors, we would have gotten a lot of complaint mail from medical or bar associations. In those days, we answered our own complaint mail, and censors never complained because they knew their complaint would just make some other censor answer the letter. At this point, I think I should tell you about "complaint" mail.

If a viewer is offended by a show, he writes a complaint letter and addresses it to William S. Paley, Chairman of the Board. If a viewer likes the show, he writes directly to Tom and Dick and tells them he likes them. So then the network only gets the complaint mail. At one time, Sam and I went to Tom and asked if we could read some of his fan mail to help us answer our complaint mail. Tom was impressed when we asked him, and almost started to talk to us on a friendly basis. Once he even bought us a drink at Kelbo's.

I should say one thing about Tom and Dick. They never cheated on any agreement we made after the Wednesday run-thru, and consequently, we never had to edit the finished tape. This helped the show as censor edits only destroy production value. Years later, Tom appreciated this. He met me at Kelbo's one night and told me so. He said he never knew that I was on his side and that he wished he had done what I said without arguments that always ended in a compromise. I told him that I agreed with him, adding that I felt if he had done so, we would still have our jobs. Tom agreed with me.

Sam Taylor, Tommy Smothers, and me at CBS

* * *

I have one more Tom Smothers story. It involves my daughter Adrienne, whom I had gotten a job as a censor on *The Merv Griffin Show* in 1972. She had just graduated from college—it was her first job in television. Metromedia was syndicating the show. One day Tom Smothers was a guest on *The Merv Griffin Show*. Adrienne was warned by the producers to stay away from Tom Smothers, whose reputation for taking censors apart was very well-known. Adrienne tried to hide, but as she was passing the makeup room, the makeup man called her in and introduced her to Tom. Apparently, the makeup man hadn't gotten the warning, or maybe he just did it for the hell of it. Tom recognized her last name and asked if Adrienne was my daughter. Adrienne told him yes. Then Tom went out and did the show. When the taping ended, Adrienne met with the producer and the director. Tommy suddenly walked into the meeting, pointed his finger at Adrienne and said, "If she wants you to take anything out, take it out. I should have done it for her father years ago." By the way, no censor edits were necessary.

CHAPTER 11

Drinking Stories

Kelbo's

Kelbo's was a Polynesian bar and restaurant across the street from CBS Television City. It was practically a CBS "company store." Interesting people frequented the bar, and sometimes interesting things happened... or maybe they didn't happen.

Franchot Tone did several *Playhouse 90* and *Climax* episodes. During show breaks, he always went to Kelbo's for a martini. Franchot was an unusual actor. I never saw him make an entrance or an exit. A number of times, when a show broke, Franchot would be on stage and some of us would walk over to Kelbo's. When we got there, Franchot would be sitting at the bar. I don't know how he beat us over because we walked fast. But there he was. Then we would look around and he was gone. No one had seen him enter or leave. When we went back to the studio, he was already on stage. None of us ever figured out how he did it.

* * *

Bob Savery was a stage manager, and a regular at Kelbo's. One night, he was holding court at the bar when somebody got a good idea, and two or three of Savery's compatriots slipped out to the parking lot. They got some water paint and painted Savery's black car white. When he went to leave, he couldn't find his car. He came back in, claiming it had been stolen. Someone told him he had walked over, and that his car was in the CBS parking lot. Savery went over to the parking lot and still couldn't find his car.

Again, he returned, claiming it had been stolen. Someone else remembered that Savery had been to the Farmer's Market, which was next to CBS, and had probably left his car there. Savery walked back to the Farmer's Market and searched for half an hour. Still no car. He came back to Kelbo's and demanded the owner call the police. Then someone else walked in and told Savery his car was in the Kelbo's parking lot. He had hosed the paint off the car ... it looked great. It was now nice and clean. By this time, Savery was sober enough to drive home. The walks had done him good. I don't know if he ever appreciated what we had done for him.

* * *

One of our newscasters—I won't mention his name— also drank at Kelbo's. He was very careful about driving after he had been drinking, and used to sit in his car and take a nap before driving home. One night, while he was napping, we went across the street to the service station, borrowed a jack and put his car up on blocks.

When he woke up, he started his car and "drove" all the way home before he figured out that he was still in the Kelbo's parking lot.

James Arness

James Arness came into Kelbo's one night after he had had a meeting with Bill Dozier. I told him I liked Dozier—that he had hired me twice and only fired me once. Jim liked Dozier, too, and he told me his Dozier story. It seems that they had tested several actors for the part of Matt Dillon on *Gunsmoke*. Jim was selected, and Dozier called him and told him to come into his office the next day and sign his contract. Jim talked to his agent and others, and was advised not to sign for a TV series. He had just had his best part in a very successful movie titled, *Hondo*. His reviews were great. He was advised that he could soon become a top motion picture star. Jim told his agent to advise Dozier of the decision.

That night, Dozier called him at home and asked him if he was really going to turn down the Matt Dillon role. Jim told Dozier that that was the advice he had been given. Dozier asked Jim if he would like some more advice. Jim said he would listen. Dozier asked Jim what he did before he became an actor. Jim said he had worked at a gas station. Dozier said, "Jim, if you don't come into my office at ten o'clock tomorrow morning and sign your *Gunsmoke* contract you'll be back pumping gas so fast you won't know what the hell happened to you." Dozier hung up the phone. Jim paused for a few moments, took a sip from his Kelbo's drink and said, "I stayed awake all night...I was very worried. At ten o'clock the next morning, I went to Dozier's office and signed my *Gunsmoke* contract." Jim paused again and took another sip, then he said, "To this day I still think Dozier was right."

Johnny Carson

In 1955, Johnny Carson had his own variety show on CBS. He frequently visited Kelbo's. One day, he was re-hearsing a sketch in which he played a Greek soldier. The carpenters had built a mock Trojan Horse, and its platform was about six feet off the floor. It was filled with Johnny and his Greek soldiers, and it was very crowded. At one point, two of the soldiers slipped off the platform and fell to the floor. Several stage hands rushed to help them back onto the platform. Johnny turned and saw them. A student of the poet, Virgil, Johnny immediately created his greatest ad lib. He warned everyone assembled on stage, "Beware of grips bearing Greeks." Virgil would have been very proud of him. His Greek soldiers were. Unfortunately, we never got it on tape, but at the next show break, they all escorted him across the street to Kelbo's, resplendent in their Greek uniforms. Each soldier bought Johnny a drink. He drank all of them. Johnny was a good drinker.

Allan Sherman

After the quiz show scandals[1], CBS cancelled all their quiz and game shows. A couple of years went by before they brought them back. The first one to be scheduled was a game show called *Your Surprise Package*. Allan Sherman was the producer, and also a Kelbo's regular. Mary Ann was a very pretty blonde girl who was a receptionist at CBS, and also a Kelbo's regular. Allan was smitten with her beauty and always wanted to kiss her. Mary Ann always refused, and said she would only kiss Allan if she were drunk. One night, Mary Ann had a few too many and somebody told Allan that Mary Ann was drunk, and would probably kiss him. Allan went over to her table, and she let him kiss her. I guess she was drunk because she then threw up all over Allan. We took him to the men's room and took off his shirt and pants. A wardrobe man took his clothes across the street to be cleaned, and brought back some clothes for him to wear home. He never tried to kiss Mary Ann again.

Allan also had a great talent for making up song parodies on the spot. Don was a CBS engineer who doubled as a piano player at Kelbo's. Sometimes Allan would

---

1 Television shows are financed by the fees that advertisers pay to the broadcast network to play their commercials during a show's broadcast. The network pays the production company to produce shows for broadcast. Those fees are commensurate with the advertising fees. The higher the audience rating, the higher the advertising fees. It was discovered that in order to boost the audience ratings of various quiz shows, the producers manipulated the outcome of the games by prompting or coaching the players. When this was discovered by the networks, many of the games were taken off the air.

walk in and tell Don to play any song he wanted. Don would start a song, and Allan would create and sing a parody while Don was playing. I remember one night Don started playing, "I Enjoy Being A Girl." Allan sang an immediate parody. People kept telling Allan that he should record these songs. Finally, somebody actually took him to Warner Brothers Records and forced him to record them. He made several albums that went gold. You may remember his album: *My Son, the Folk Singer.*

Chuck Jones

Animator Chuck Jones was a CBS regular. In the late 50's, he bought his first Volkswagen. He kept careful records, and was thrilled when he found out that he was getting better than thirty miles to the gallon. He kept telling everyone about his car until we all grew sick of listening to him. Then someone had a good idea. We would take turns buying a gallon jug of gas and pouring it into his gas tank in the Kelbo's parking lot. His mileage kept going up … he started to get forty miles to the gallon, then fifty, and finally a little better than sixty. And he talked about his car even more. Finally, we got a rubber hose and siphoned the gas back out of the tank about two or three times a week. His mileage started to drop to fifty, to forty, and finally it was well under thirty. He then started taking it back to the dealer for checkups, and he started to drive the dealer crazy. Finally, the story got out, and Chuck learned what we had been doing. He shut up about his car … the plan had worked beautifully.

Joe Frisco And The Masquer's Club

Joe Frisco, the stuttering night-club comic, had been an old friend of Dad's. When I came to Hollywood, Joe was working on and off at Charlie Foy's Supper Club, and every once in a while I'd run into him. I especially remember one night at the Masquer's Club[2] in Hollywood. The Masquer's was fundamentally an actors' club, although producers, writers, and directors were also members. One regular was Captain Horace Brown who had married Marion Davies after William Randolph Hearst had died.

On this particular night, Joe walked up to the bar with a twenty-dollar bill which he threw down on the bar. He ordered himself a scotch and soda and told the bartender, "S-s-s-see what my fr-fr-fr-friends will have," and walked away, leaving the twenty. The bartender set up the drinks for the bar and took the twenty. Joe very seldom had money ... he was usually broke. But when he had money, he always shared it with his friends, and he expected them to do the same with him.

About ten minutes later, Joe came back with another twenty and ordered another round. We started to wonder from where he was getting the twenties, and when he returned later with another twenty and ordered

---

2 The Masquer's Club was an organization of Broadway stars and entertainers who lived in the Hollywood area. Described as a sort of fraternity, The Masquer's Club was a meeting-place for the rich and famous in Hollywood, catering to the social elite. The organization was founded in 1927 with members that included Jack Benny and Cary Grant.

another round of drinks, I asked him where he was get-ting the money from. He told me, "Fr-fr-fr-from that g-g-guy who married that g-g-girl whose b-b-boyfriend used to s-s-sell n-n-n-newspapers." We then knew that Horace Brown was giving Joe the twenties, but we were somewhat amazed at Joe's regard for the late William Randolph Hearst.

CHAPTER 12

Red Skelton

W HEN I FIRST joined Program Practices, I was assigned to the *Red Skelton Show*. There had been a mix up on an episode in which Mae West was the guest star, and my boss decided to change editors. Fortunately, I had become a friend of Cecil Barker, the producer, who advised me to keep out of Red's way. I did what he told me, and remained assigned to the show for years. Red was probably the most talented comedian I had ever seen. Some entertainers could take an audience and make them laugh. Others could take an audience and make them cry. Skelton could do both, and could even switch directions in the middle of a routine. I'm not sure if I've ever met a real genius in my lifetime. If I haven't, Red is the closest I've come.

Skelton and Paley

Periodically, William S. Paley, Chairman of the Board of CBS, visited Television City in Hollywood to touch base with his branch office employees. He usually brought an entourage which walked behind him in order of their importance. One year, I think it was 1963, he walked onto Stage 33 where Red Skelton was rehearsing. He was followed in order by Dr. Frank Stanton, Vice Chairman of the Board; James T. Aubrey, President of the Television Network; Guy della Cioppa, Vice President Programs—CBS Hollywood; and James Hesen, Director of Building Facilities.

Red broke rehearsal, shook hands with Mr. Paley, and they talked for a few seconds. Red then decided to liven up the formal proceedings. He called over Willie Dahl, his stage manager, introduced him to Mr. Paley and then said, "Willie, tell Mr. Paley what you just said about his goddamned network." A hush fell over the entourage but it didn't bother Willie. He patted the Chairman of the Board on the shoulder and said, "Mr. Paley, you got a good thing going for ya ... don't fuck it up." A hush fell over the entourage. Mr. Paley stared at Willie for a few beats. Then he started to laugh. Dr. Stanton saw Paley laugh, so he laughed. Aubrey saw Stanton laugh, so he laughed. Della Cioppa saw Aubrey laugh, so he laughed. Hesen saw della Cioppa laugh, so he laughed. There was then a huge sigh of relief throughout the studio. A major crisis had been averted and the pecking order had been maintained.

Red Skelton and Jackie Coogan

Red Skelton had always taped his television show at Television City. But one year he decided to buy his own studio as an investment. He bought the old Charlie

Chaplin Studio near the corner of Sunset Boulevard and La Brea, and converted it into a television facility. He taped his own show there, and also leased the studio out to other producers. One night, while he was rehearsing his show, the main brace across the ceiling started to collapse. Some of the lights fell to the floor and we all rushed outside. Jackie Coogan was standing beside me, looking up at the building. Finally, he turned to me and said, "You know, forty years ago when Chaplin built that stage, I told him that the main brace wasn't strong enough. As you can see, I was right."

Skelton's Last Show

While doing his last show of the season, the announcement came through that he would not continue on CBS next season. At two o'clock on Tuesdays, Red always did a camera run-thru with no audience. On this particular Tuesday, someone took Red out of the building for lunch. When he returned a few minutes late and walked onto the stage, they pulled the curtain and the usually empty audience section was filled with every CBS employee that could fit in the studio. We gave him a standing ovation which lasted several minutes. Red was really appreciative. Tears came to his eyes, and he thanked everyone from the bottom of his heart. He noticed me standing in the back and said, "Gee, even Pettijohn, the censor, came to see me." Mine was the only name that he mentioned, and it made me very proud.

Red Skelton and celebrity guests at FDR's Birthday Ball

A Note From Adrienne

As many parents take their kids to work on occasion, Dad did the same with his. One day when I was little, I was standing outside of the stage door entrance to the Red Skelton Show *while Dad was talking to someone nearby. There were about five steps leading up to the door's entrance and Mr. Skelton was sitting on them. So I decided to join him, and sat down next to him. We didn't say much to each other, just sat together looking around. When my Dad turned around and saw this, he quickly called me to join him. He told me that Mr. Skelton was a very private man and that I should never do anything like that again. And while I wasn't sure what "a private man" was, I now understood why we didn't say much to each other when we were sitting on the steps.*

CHAPTER 13

Carol Burnett

O F ALL THE television stars I ever met, without
a doubt, the most professional, the most talented, and the most gracious was Carol Burnett.
She was never late, always knew her lines, and always
knew the name of everyone on the crew. She probably
also knew the names of their wives, their children, and I
think she also knew what schools the children attended.
She never forgot a name.

Carol Burnett and the "Huskies"

The "Huskies" were from Seattle, Washington. They
were members of the University of Washington Huskies
Fan Club, and they came to Hollywood once a year
when their football team played USC or UCLA. They
were two middle-aged married couples. One couple was
Fred and Lois, the other was Frank and Ruthie. They
always stayed at the motel across the street from CBS
Television City, and they always frequented the motel
bar. That explains how I met them. When they found
out I worked on *The Carol Burnett Show* they were

thrilled. I think they almost liked Carol Burnett better than their football team. I promised to take them across the street to meet Carol and to watch one of her rehearsals. I mentioned that Carol sometimes came over to the motel bar for a sandwich during show breaks.

The night before I was to take them over to rehearsal, Frank and Ruthie got in a minor argument, and Frank got huffy and walked out. He came back in about an hour and a half, and we told him that Carol had come over while he was gone and had had a sandwich with us. Frank didn't believe a word of it. The next day I took them over to the stage.

I had told Carol the story of the night before and she was delighted to go along with it. She asked their names and remembered them. During a break in rehearsal, she came down off the stage, went to Fred, Lois, and Ruthie, called them by name, and said how much she'd enjoyed meeting them the night before. She then turned to Frank and said, "You must be Frank. We missed you last night. I'm sorry you couldn't be there." For the rest of his life, Frank was never sure whether or not Carol had come into the bar the night before, and none of us were ever going to tell him.

Ross Murray's Eggs

One season there was a technicians' strike at CBS. The network executives had to fill in for the engineers doing jobs they knew nothing about. I ended up as the sound effects man on *The Carol Burnett Show*. I was very bad at the job. A lot of my friends were technicians, and I feel my poor standard of work had a lot to do with an early settlement of the strike.

Once, during *The Carol Burnett Show*, Dave Powers, the director, needed a mushy "plop" sound. I looked in Ross Murray's sound effects locket—Ross was the regular sound effects man—but I couldn't find any such effect. Then someone suggested dropping a hardboiled egg on a board beside the sound effects microphone. My assistant, Harry Zipper, went to the cafeteria and got six hard-boiled eggs. The sound effect worked on the first take and Harry put the other five eggs in Ross' locker.

About a month after the strike was settled, Ross sent me the five eggs through the inter-office mail with a cover memo. I could smell them coming down the hall before they arrived. I immediately sent them on to Harry Zipper through the inter-office mail with a cover memo. After all, they were his eggs. He, too, smelled them coming long before they got there. I guess he threw them out.

Harvey Meets the President

In 1969, Bob Wood became President of CBS Television Network. I ran into him in the hall while I was on my way to a *Carol Burnett* rehearsal. He was on his way to say hello to Carol, and we walked down together. On the way down, we ran into Joan, a secretary in the Law Department. She was carrying a long blonde wig, and Bob asked to borrow it. He put it on and we slipped backstage. Harvey Korman, and Carol were rehearsing a sketch in their apartment set. Bob Duggan, a bit player, was outside the door awaiting a cue to enter and deliver a telegram. Bob Wood took Bob Duggan's telegram and his place by the door. He entered on cue wearing the wig, and handed Carol the telegram. Carol burst out laughing but Harvey didn't. He complained about the rehearsal being interrupted. Carol then introduced Harvey to the new President of the network, and Harvey's attitude changed immediately. Later, Harvey was worried that he might have done something to offend Bob. He bawled me out for not tipping him off. Harvey said he didn't know who Bob Wood was or what he did. Carol came to my rescue. She told Harvey not to worry because Bob didn't know who Harvey was or what he did, either. Harvey was not too happy with Carol's explanation—but we all have a touch of vanity.

The CBS Golf Tournament

The CBS Employees Club had a couple of golf tournaments a year, and we had a regular foursome that always played together. It consisted of the producer of *The Carol Burnett Show,* Joe Hamilton, who was also Carol's husband; Harvey Korman, her co-star; Pat Kenney, one of her cameramen; and me.

One weekend, the tournament was held at Singing Hills, just outside of San Diego. When the show finished taping on Friday night, Pat and I drove to San Diego and got a motel room. Our starting time was ten o'clock Saturday morning, but Joe and Harvey decided to drive down early Saturday. They planned to drop their wives off at a resort hotel more suitable than a motel room. Pat and I were on the first tee at ten o'clock, and they still hadn't shown up. Suddenly, there was a screech of tires as Joe wheeled his Rolls Royce through the parking lot up to the first tee. Harvey took their clubs and shoes out of the trunk, and Joe drove off to park the car.

Harvey apologized for being late, but said it was Joe's fault. He explained that they had plenty of time to get there, but Joe insisted on speeding. Harvey said he told Joe not to speed, but Joe wouldn't listen to him. Sure enough, a motorcycle officer stopped them and started to write Joe a ticket. Then he looked over and saw Harvey and recognized him. Harvey said the cop was a big fan of his, and stopped writing the ticket, letting Joe off with a warning. Joe walked back to the first tee and told us a slightly different story. He claimed that the cop that pulled him over was a car buff and simply wanted to talk to him about the Rolls Royce. He and the cop were getting along fine until Harvey, the "ham" actor, interrupted them by saying he was a big television star, and the cop had no right to hold him up. Harvey was very obnoxious, and the cop got mad and started to write a ticket. He had never heard of Harvey and asked for the car registration. Then Joe said, "Thank God the car was registered in Carol's name. He had never heard of Harvey but he was a big fan of Carol's. He let me off with a warning." Pat and I could never find the cop, so we don't know the true story.

A Final Note from Adrienne

IN THE EARLY 1970s, Dad was offered a promotion to Vice President of the CBS Program Practices department. It would have required relocating back to New York. In those days, zipping back and forth on weekends wasn't as common (except in the case of the Smothers Brothers Show) as it is today. Moreover, he would no longer have been interacting on a daily basis with his closest friends—his show biz buddies. So my father decided not to accept the promotion, and to remain in California.

Dad retired from CBS about a year later. He continued to consult on various shows, but I think he just enjoyed "schmoozing with his buds"!

David, Muffy and I followed in Grandpa's and Dad's footsteps. Not only did David and Muffy golf, but David went into the show biz industry and became an audio editor. He won an Emmy for his work on the first television mini-series, *Roots*. His audio work on the film, *E.T. Extra Terrestrial* won an Oscar. My sister had a brief television career at CBS. During the transition from black and white TV broadcasting to color, she was as important as the cameras. You see, she was the color model on which the cameras were adjusted to match one another prior to broadcasting a television show. Like Grandma Helen, she gave up "show biz" when she got married. When she left, CBS replaced her with Zelda, a mannequin which is in use to this day!

Muffy at CBS

When I finished college, I wanted to continue my education and get my teaching credentials. My father suggested that I accept a three month position as the "censor" on *The Merv Griffin Show*, after which I could return to school if I still wanted to become a teacher. I accepted Dad's "challenge" knowing full well he'd lose and I'd get to go back to school. Well, it's been well over forty years, and I'm still in the "biz."

Like Grandpa, Dad was smarter than everyone. I just didn't know it at the time. And like Grandpa, my father's career kept him away from home a lot. On weekends, when he was home, he slept, went to the club to play golf, and watched sports in the living room. The family did assemble occasionally for Sunday dinner, at which time it was a free-for-all with everyone talking at once. However, at the dinner table, us kids thought our stories were more important than Dad's were. So in the mid-1970s, when he asked me to type his stories as he dictated them, it was really the first time I learned about the Pettijohn family history. I was astounded by my father's upbringing. While typing up the stories, I would ask Dad questions, but Dad was very casual about everything, and thought the stories were self-explanatory. He was very quiet about his life and upbringing. I didn't meet his brother, the New York Attorney General, until I was thirteen. Uncle Bruce didn't talk about his adventures either. Most of what I know about my family is from helping my father write this book. And boy, does it impress the hell out of me!

About the Authors

Charles C. Pettijohn was born in New York in 1918. A golf star at a young age, Pettijohn attended Georgetown University. After college he and his wife moved to Hollywood. Pettijohn took a job with the Motion Picture Production Code Board, and then went on to a career as a writer and a production executive with CBS. After retiring in the early 1970s, he found time to write a diary about some of his greatest adventures.

Adrienne Pettijohn graduated from UC Berkeley and immediately began work on *The Merv Griffin Show* as the network censor. Since then she has worked for more than forty years in the entertainment industry, working in game shows, music variety shows, soap operas, sitcoms, and the news.

She was a producer for the popular game show *Win, Lose or Draw* and worked at the Walt Disney Studio's Home Entertainment, helping the company transition from video to DVD, Blu-Ray, and video streaming. Adrienne is a member of the Director's Guild of America and has written two screenplays.